Blowing Away the State Writing Assessment Test

Blowing Away the State Writing Assessment Test

Four Steps to Better Scores for Teachers of All Levels

Second Edition

Jane Bell Kiester

Blowing Away the State Writing Assessment Test
Four steps to better scores for teachers of all levels

Jane Bell Kiester

Cover design: *Maria Messenger*
Layout design: *Billie J. Hermansen*

Order Maupin House Books directly at 1-800-524-0634 or 352-373-5588
E-mail for faster service: info@maupinhouse.com or visit www.maupinhouse.com.

Maupin House
PO Box 90148
Gainesville, FL 32607
Fax: 352-373-5546

Kiester, Jane Bell, 1945-
    Blowing away the state writing assessment test : four steps to better scores for teachers
of all levels / Jane Bell Kiester.
        p. cm.
    Includes bibliographical references ( ).
    ISBN 0-929895-36-3
    1. English language--Composition and exercises--Evaluation. 2. English
language--Examinations.
LB1576.K473 2000
808'.042'076--dc21   00-025529

Dedicated to the memory of my father, James F. Bell (1914-1995), esteemed professor, experimentist, physicist, Renaissance man, historian, writer, musician, encourager of and inspiration for daughter, and Daddy Extraordinaire.

I miss you.

Acknowledgments

There are two people in my life without whom I could never write--my husband, Charles L. Kiester and my mother, Perra S. Bell. These two tireless, mostly uncomplaining editors read this book again and again, made invaluable (and sometimes sweeping) suggestions, corrected my errors, encouraged me when I was tired of working, put up with visiting with the back of my head, loved me even when I was grumpy from hours at the computer, and kept me honest. My husband also terses me up, keeping my books of readable length. You two are the best mom and husband in the world. I love you both.

I would also like to thank some of my colleagues for their help in producing this book. We are all in this teaching business together, and I, for one, couldn't survive without their encouragement, suggestions, and support.

Catherine Berg, the ninth-grade teacher and friend who encouraged me to write the first *Caught'ya* book, also read this one. Without her input on the needs of high school students, this book would not have been as accurate.

Mary Ann Coxe, also a colleague and friend (and head of English for Alachua County, Florida), who encouraged me to write that first book six years ago, read this manuscript from the point of view of a supervisor, a former high school teacher, and an official scorer of the Florida State Writing Assessment. She managed (once again) to zero in on the one thing that bothered me about the manuscript and made suggestions that improved it greatly. Thanks, again, Mary Ann.

Renée Trufant has been a dear friend for over twenty years when my six-year-old son won her heart at the check-out line at Publix Supermarket where she was working. We have been fast friends ever since, although I did influence her to become a middle-school teacher instead of a lawyer. She tells me that she is very happy as a teacher. I know she experiences great success. Her students' State Writing Assessment scores are very high. Her students love her. And, she has dynamite (and often wonderfully bizarre) ideas. Her contribution to this book is no exception. Thank you, Renée, for letting me pick your brain for ideas for this book. Thank you also for all the long-distance brainstorming.

Tim McShane, fellow eighth-grade English teacher at Westwood Middle School, and author of *Boston Baked Bean* and *The Votive Pit,* among other plays, also read the manuscript, made valuable suggestions, and encouraged me to finish this book despite my desire to work on my fiction.

Jim Owens, a tenth-grade teacher, kindly let me into his students' folders and allowed me to purloin examples for the last section of this book. He also has provided frequent and enthusiastic encouragement for my writing.

Amy Rollo, a fourth-grade teacher, read the manuscrcript and made some very helpful suggestions. She also lent me examples her students wrote so that I could use them in the last section of this book.

And, finally, I wish again to thank Maupin House for believing in me enough to keep publishing and marketing my books. A better, more author-friendly, publishing company could not be found.

Contents

Introduction

As of this edition, thirty-nine states have instituted a writing assessment test. It does not matter whether these tests are scored on a one-to-four scale, a one-to-five scale, or a one-to-six scale: they are all scored holistically using essentially the same criteria. A top paper is a top paper, whether that score is a four, a five, or a six. All thirty-nine states require the same types of writing, although some ask for two, some three, or all four of them. These writing genres include narrative and three types of essays — the expository (explanatory, clarification), the persuasive (point of view), and/or the descriptive. Again, the basic criteria for each type of essay are essentially the same, no matter what grade level is being tested, no matter what state.

Most states test students in the fourth, eighth, and tenth grades, but a few vary by a grade level or so. Again, the grade level tested does not affect the scoring process. A great expository/clarification essay at the elementary level is as good as (albeit less sophisticated) a great essay at the high-school level. A poor example of an essay is terrible and incoherent no matter the grade level. (See the examples at the end of the book and compare the fourth-grade and tenth-grade papers.)

This is why this book, although written by a Florida teacher whose students face and ace the Florida Writes Test, is generic enough to be effective in any state at any level — elementary, middle, or high. All four types of writing are addressed, and the examples of student writing (located at the end of the book) can be used with students at all grade levels. The techniques and strategies suggested in this book address how to get your students to write well whether under the pressure of a test or simply writing in the classroom for their teacher. These techniques have worked in classrooms all over the country. A bit of history is in order at this point.

In August, 1993, before school even started, I was already terribly worried about the writing-test scores of that year's students. We had been told that the returned scores would be listed by teacher and by class. This made me doubly nervous. That same year the powers-that-be had done away with compensatory education and drop-out prevention classes in the eighth grade. In addition, all the gifted students had been pulled out of my English classes and placed in a special gifted humanities course.

In my not-quite-heterogeneous classes would be placed one-half of those students who so lacked English skills that their Stanines were less than **2.2** in language arts on the California Achievement Test. Thus, my class average on the Florida Writes Test would not include the top scores that some of the gifted students were capable of earning to average with the lower scores of those students who found it difficult to write a simple sentence. I was very worried!

I called Renée Trufant, a friend who teaches in North Carolina. She is a wonderfully exciting teacher as well as a dear friend, and she had had a state writing assessment test to contend with several years before Florida instituted ours. I remembered hearing her moan (long-distance) about the test, but I also remembered that she had told me her students had scored particularly well. I picked her brains for hours. My long distance bill that month was hideous, but it didn't matter. Renée shared the teaching techniques she felt had helped her students obtain high scores on the North Carolina State Writing Assessment Test.

Next, I called Mary Ann Coxe, the head of English in our county, to cry on her shoulder. Mary Ann always has ideas up her sleeve. Although she has been our administrator for years, she is still an English teacher to the core of her being. She threw into the pot more theories-for-successful-test-scores.

I also brainstormed with a fellow eighth-grade English teacher at my middle school for his suggestions. Tim McShane, never short of great ideas about writing and a writer himself, added his own panache to the solution.

I was then ready to develop a plan. I devised a four-step plan, cautiously implemented this plan in my classes, and anxiously waited for the test results. It worked! That year, the average score of eighth graders in the state of Florida was **2.7** on a scale of zero to six. The county eighth-grade average was **2.8**. My students' scores, even with all those former non-writers included, averaged **3.4**! Success!

Out of 83 students in my English classes (I teach French also), the lowest score was **1.5** (and there was only one of these). A half-a-dozen scored 5's. One student achieved a **6**! **The bottom line was that 82% scored above the district and the state average.** Needless to say I was thrilled! Many of my poorest students had received above-average scores.

Four years ago, I began to teach gifted students. Recalling that the "gifted" label does not mean that the child necessarily is "gifted" in writing, I again implemented the four-step program. In fact, at the beginning of the year, a few of my gifted students wrote only slightly better than some of the compensatory students I had taught the previous year.

Despite these students and despite the one gifted student who received a score of **0** because he refused to write for the "establishment" (typical gifted behavior), the average score was **4.6** on a six-point scale! This same average has continued for the past few years culminating with last year when thirty percent of my students earned a **5.5** (twenty-one of them), or a **6** (nine of them), with the lowest score a **3.5** (only two of them).

Using the ideas in this book, my colleagues also spur their students to earn consistently high scores. With demographics that would predict a below-average score, our school's eighth grade continues to maintain a school average of **3.9** or **4.0** on the Florida Writes Test. This is higher than all the elementary and middle schools and most of the high schools in the county. In a rural county sixty miles away, a high-school teacher of the drop-out prevention program used the first edition of this book. His students earned higher scores (averaging a **3.7**) than the advanced students in his school! The method works!

With this year's students, I again am implementing the four-step program. What is this successful system that evokes average scores from students with below-average skills in English and the highest scores from many of the others?

Read on.... Whether you teach elementary, middle, or high school; whether you teach in Florida, North Carolina, Wisconsin, California, **or any other state**, follow these four steps to higher scores.

STEP ONE

Teach Students to Write Strong-verb Practice Paragraphs

1. Introduction to the Strong Verbs

The first step to blowing away your state's writing test involves teachers in the grade levels before yours. To get the highest scores possible from your students, you need to convince your colleagues of *all* disciplines in at least one but preferably two grade levels below yours to start teaching their students to write strong-verb paragraphs. Even second- and third-grade students can be taught to write these paragraphs! High school students groan and protest, but they, too, need the practice. I am firmly convinced that our school's above-average scores on the state writing assessment test are due in part because the English teachers at all three grade levels assign strong-verb paragraphs to their students.

Even if you cannot convince your colleagues to work with their students on this, you can begin having your students write these paragraphs the second week of school, and they will be well prepared in time for the test. Learning to write strong-verb paragraphs is crucial because they are a microcosm of the essays required on the test in that they have a beginning, a middle with detail, and an end. In addition, **strong verbs = better writing = higher scores**. You may have noticed in literature that helping verbs are

sparingly used. Instead, vivid, "showing," **active** verbs abound in descriptions. Your students, no matter at what age level, can learn to write similarly.

In the strong-verb paragraphs each of the parts (introduction or beginning, detail, conclusion) is a sentence or two rather than a paragraph, but your students get the hang of the general format that they will follow when writing an expository or persuasive essay or a description in a narrative story. (See **Step Three** for an explanation of a basic essay and story.) With the strong-verb paragraphs, you also can introduce the idea of using similes in their writing, a sure-fire score raiser.

What I call strong-verb paragraphs actually are artificially-constructed paragraphs based on Rebakah Caplan's idea of Showing Writing (*Showing Writing. A Training Program to Help Students.* Berkeley: University of California Press, 1980). Before you begin assigning these paragraphs to your students, however, those of you at the middle or elementary levels might want to have a little fun as you prepare your students to enthusiastically use strong verbs in their writing. Since these paragraphs are difficult to write and require some thought on the part of the writer, student enthusiasm is important. High school teachers can use a challenge to charge their students.

To introduce the concept of strong (action) verb usage, a teacher with a sense of drama gets the point across most effectively. The more drama used, the better the retention of the lesson. Students remember the unusual. With these maxims in mind, I used to introduce the use of strong verbs over helping verbs in the following manner. (Now the sixth grade teachers at my school do this.) In elementary and high schools, second and ninth grade respectively can have the honor.

On a pre-announced day, my students and I dressed in lugubrious clothes, made tiny coffins, put a list of the helping verbs to avoid (the "dead verbs") inside, and held a mock funeral. Some students made a headstone out of cardboard. We all solemnly walked to the edge of the campus, singing a sad rendition of the tune "The Volga Boatman" with the "dead verbs" as the words. Here is the list.

Verbs to Bury (Dead Verbs)

am	have
are	is
be	was
had	were
has	any verb ending in "ing"

(Upper grades should also avoid "feels," "looks," "sounds," "smells," "becomes," "seems," and "acts.")

As we dug a hole with my husband's reluctantly-lent best shovel and buried the coffins containing the "dead verbs," each student delivered a brief eulogy to the "dead verb" (usually "is" or "was") that he/she used the most. Upon completion of the "funeral," we returned to the classroom and made a bulletin board that depicted a gravestone with the "dead verbs" listed on it. This board served as a reference for students for the rest of the year. After that day,

students were to avoid the "dead verbs" in their writing as much as possible. Although the sixth-grade teachers in my school have now taken up my shovel, and I no longer go through the drama of burying the "dead verbs" with my students, I still put up that bulletin board as a reminder, and we sing the "Volga Boatman's Song" on a daily basis for at least a month. We do this early in the year. In fact, I begin practicing the use of strong verbs in August. It starts the year off right with a song and a laugh.

High-school teachers whose students may have been writing such paragraphs for years, still can require a weekly practice of writing a strong-verb paragraph to keep their students in shape. They really improve writing.

2. Introducing Students to the Use of Strong Verbs

After the drama and the introduction which tell students which verbs to avoid, the next step is to introduce students to strong verbs and demonstrate how to substitute them for the "dead verbs" that they ordinarily use when they write. You will do this with sentence writing. Those of you who teach Honors English at the high-school level and whose students already may have mastered the art of using active verbs in their writing may still want to spend a day practicing with the sentences. High-school students in regular classes definitely need the review. To this end, I have included a second **Practice Sheet** just for high school students. It contains more serious and thought-provoking sentences than those on the worksheet for elementary- and middle-school students.

Strong verbs are action verbs which show what is going on. "Students **shouted** invectives at the top of their lungs" is a good example of strong verb usage. Most students would have written "Students were shouting invectives," a much weaker sentence.

Students usually write what Rebakah Caplan calls "telling" sentences such as the following: "The puppy is cute," or "I am bored." They do not naturally write sentences that "show" what they are trying to say and provide support for the topic sentence. For example: "The cute puppy **wriggles** in excitement whenever someone comes in the door." "I **twiddle** my thumbs out of boredom." These good "showing" sentences illustrate just how cute the puppy is and how bored I am. Much more powerful writing results from the use of strong verbs.

> **NOTE:** *Lower grades or schools with large numbers of students whose vocabulary skills are not up to par will want to keep a list of alternative verbs prominently posted in the classroom. Perhaps this list could be elicited from the students themselves.*

Teacher and students together should write strong verb sentences, a few a day, with the verbs elicited from the students. Begin with a "telling" sentence that uses a "dead" verb. Change the sentence into a "showing" one. Practice with sentences like those on the **Strong-verb Sentence Practice Sheets** (see following pages) or with sentences culled from you students' papers. Students need to become accustomed to writing active rather than passive sentences. At first it is awkward for them, but it is important to wait for students' responses as it usually takes children a little while to catch on to the idea. Feel free to copy these sheets for use in your classroom. The sentences I provide here are only suggestions, and most are very general.

Elementary and middle school teachers may want to assign their students to work on the practice sheet in pairs or groups of three or four. High school teachers can assign it to students individually and then share the results.

Strong-verb Sentence Practice Sheet

(for Primary Grades and for introduction purposes at any level)

1. The cat _____ in the chair.

2. A big brown dog _____ at the little cat.

3. The big dog then _____ the cat around the house.

4. My teacher _____ when the class talks too much.

5. Rabbits _____ when they smell danger.

6. The smelly, black and white skunk _____ on the

    dog when the dog _____ it.

7. Our teacher _____ us how to write.

8. A yellow ball _____ down the stairs.

9. I _____ my best friend.

10. My friend _____ to school with me.

11. A big blue bird _____ in the window.

12. When the teacher _____, I _____ .

Possible (but not the only) Answers to
Primary Strong-verb Practice Sentences

1. The cat **curled up** in the chair.
    (sat, yawned, slept, etc.)

2. A big brown dog **barked** at the little cat.
    (growled, whined, etc.)

3. The big dog then **chased** the cat around the house.
    (pursued, followed, etc.)

4. My teacher **frowns** when the class **talks** too much.
    (yells, sighs, shouts, etc.)   **(chatters, prattles, etc.)**

5. Rabbits **run** when they **smell** danger.
    (scamper off, quiver in fear, etc.)   **(sense, notice, etc.)**

6. The smelly, black and white skunk **sprayed** the dog when the dog
    attacked it.
    (peed on, bit, etc.)   **(growled at, chased, etc.)**

7. Our teacher **teaches** us how to write.
    (shows, demonstrates to, etc.)

8. A yellow ball **bounced** down the stairs.
    (rolled, fell, etc.)

9. I **hugged** my best friend.
    (love, played with, etc.)

10. My friend **walked** to school with me.
    (ambled, skipped, came, etc.)

11. A big blue bird **tapped on** the window.
    (pecked at, hit, etc.)

12. When the teacher **talks**, I **listen**.
    (yells, teaches, etc.)   **(learn, cringe, pay attention, etc.)**

Strong-verb Sentence Practice Sheet

(for Elementary Schools)

NOTE — The key is to show just how lonely, sad, happy, etc. the person is by telling something he or she would do. What do you do when you are sad? mad? happy? lonely?

1. The boy *was* lonely.

2. The little girl *was* sad.

3. The girl in the red dress *was* happy.

4. My teacher *is* slightly crazy and lots of fun.

5. My mom *is* mad at me.

6. My friend *is* mean to his sister.

7. These sentences *are* stupid.

8. The calico cat was a nice cat.

9. The little dog with the floppy ears *was* cute.

10. When I go to my grandparents' house, I *am* happy.

11. School *is* sometimes boring.

12. My room *is* a mess.

13. She *is* my best friend, and we *have* fun together.

14. The sky *is* blue with lots of fluffy clouds.

15. There are nasty brown roaches in my backpack.

16. The classroom *was* noisy

17. The birthday party *was* awesome.

18. The skunk *is* smelly.

19. I am mad today.

20. It was fun.

Several Possible (but not the only) Answers to the Elementary Practice Sentences

1. The lonely boy **sat** in the corner and **cried**.
   The lonely boy **played** all by himself.

2. The sad little girl **cried** piteously.
   The sad little girl **ran** to her mother and **sobbed** in her arms.

3. The girl in the red dress **danced** with joy.
   The girl in the red dress **twirled** around the room from happiness.

4. My crazy, fun teacher **plays** with us on the jungle gym.
   My crazy, fun teacher **likes** skunks.

5. My mom sometimes **yells** at me angrily.
   My angry mom **puts** me in my room when I **do** something bad.

6. My friend **hits** and **teases** his sister.
   My friend **takes** his sister's dolls and **breaks** them.

7. These stupid sentences **take** a long time to do.
   These stupid sentences **teach** me about strong verbs.

8. The nice calico cat **licked** my hand.
   The nice calico cat **curled up** in my lap and **purred**.

9. The cute little dog with the floppy ears **chased** its tail.
   The cute little dog with the floppy ears **rolled** on its back and **waved** its paws in the air.

10. When I go to my grandparents' house, I **get** anything I ask for.
    I **love** going to my grandparents' house because they **play** with me and **love** me a lot.

11. School **bores** me when I **must do** worksheets.
    Doing math problems **puts** me to sleep.

12. My clothes **litter** the floor of my messy room.
    In my messy room clothes **cover** the floor and math papers **spill out of** the thr trash can.

13. My best friend and I **play** games together all the time.
    My best friend and I **visit** each other's houses every day.

NOTE — Sometimes you need to reverse the parts of the sentence.

14. Lots of fluffy clouds **dot** the blue sky.
    Lots of fluffy clouds **float** in the beautiful blue sky overhead.

15. Nasty brown roaches **live** in my backpack.
    Nasty brown roaches **eat** my lunch in my backpack.

16. The noisy classroom **hummed** with students at their learning centers.
    The students **talked**, **shouted** at each other, and **laughed** happily as they
    played in the noisy classroom.

17. We **stayed** up late at the awesome birthday party.
    A clown and lots of animals **came** to the awesome birthday party.

18. The smelly skunk **sprayed on** the mean kid.
    The smelly skunk still **reeked** from spraying a dog.

NOTE — Sometimes you may want to take a totally different tack that doesn't even mention the adjective, just demonstrates it with action.

19. In my anger, I **want** to hit and yell at everyone today.
    My face **frowns** and **scrunches** up in anger.

20. My hair **stood** on end, and I **laughed** and **screamed** on the roller coaster ride.
    At Disney World, we **rode** on lots of rides and **met** Mickey Mouse.

Strong-verb Sentence Practice Sheet

(for Middle Schools)

Directions:

Change the following "dead" verb sentences into strong ones that make vivid images that you can see. Paint word pictures with your sentences. You must include all the information in the original sentence. You may add more information if you wish. Note the verb tense of the "telling" sentence. You can see **Possible Answers to the Elementary Practice Sentences** for more ideas and examples.

Example:

"Dead" verb sentence — She was angry.
Strong verb sentence — The angry girl **flung** her arms about in frustration.

1. He has a long nose that is blue and is ugly.

2. My friend is mean to me.

3. The girl has long, stringy hair that hangs past her shoulders.

4. The teacher is totally crazy.

5. There are nasty brown roaches in my backpack.

6. There are always lots of students in the hallways of school.

7. I know my teacher is happy because she has a big smile on her face.

8. The boy in the corner is lonely.

9. The music was wonderful and had a great melody.

10. The monster has bulb-like purple eyes popping out of its head.

11. The young lady is a real loud-mouth.

12. We were the best in the class that day.

13. English teachers are always asking us to read something.

14. The adorable kitten is very playful.

15. The party was awesome.

16. The skunk was smelly. (Discourage the use of the verb "smell.")

Strong-verb Sentence Practice Sheet

(for High Schools)

Directions:

Change the following "dead" verb sentences into strong ones that make vivid images that you can see. Paint word pictures with your sentences. You must include all the information in the original sentence. You may add more information if you wish. Note the verb tense of the "telling" sentence.

Example:

"Dead" verb sentence — She was angry.
Strong verb sentence — The angry girl **flung** her arms about in frustration.

1. The halls were crowded with chattering students.

2. He was terribly lonely at home on a Saturday evening.

3. Shakespeare's play "Romeo and Juliet" is a tragedy.

4. When she broke up with her boyfriend, the girl was sad and depressed.

5. The high school's football team was great!

6. America was in a state of turmoil during the Civil War.

7. The Renaissance was a period of great creativity.

8. Shakespeare had a way with words.

9. The boy was guilty of a misdemeanor.

10. She looked guilty.

11. We have too much homework.

12. Drinking alcohol and then driving a car is dangerous.

13. He was depressed about his grades.

14. Love is a many-splendored thing.

15. He was green with envy.

16. Requiring two years of a foreign language for college is _____.

3. Introducing the Paragraphs and Some Topic Sentences to Use

Once students can successfully write strong-verb sentences on their own, and can change the sentences on the worksheet(s), they are ready to write the paragraphs. A strong-verb paragraph is a paragraph that, if possible, is composed of as many sentences as the grade level you teach, though it is not good to go below four nor above nine. The first sentence is a "telling" one, a topic sentence with a "dead" verb. The teacher supplies this sentence. (Please note that you may wish to ask your students to change this topic sentence to a "grabber.") The last sentence is a conclusion. It cannot be a repeat of the first sentence but can be similar. It may also contain a "dead" verb since it wraps things up. The sentences in the middle must all support the topic sentence and must use only strong verbs, none of which may be used more than once.

Before students are ready to write a strong-verb paragraph on their own, it is a good idea for the entire class to contribute to writing jointly a few paragraphs on the overhead or board. You provide only the topic sentence. I always write on the overhead, taking dictation from my students. They enjoy this. High-school teachers may wish to have students work on the first few paragraphs of the year in pairs or groups of three or four and skip the exercise of writing as a whole class. Topic sentences that have proven to be popular with students include the following:

Elementary and Middle Schools:

The students in the cafeteria were wild.
He/She looks weird.
My little brother (sister, cousin, etc.) is a pain.
I was very happy.
My room is a mess.
The old man was lonely.
The party was awesome!
My teacher is strange.
My mom makes me angry.
School is boring (exciting).
The classroom was noisy.
My teachers are mean!

High School:

The party was awesome.
The students were impossible for the substitute.
The last football (basketball, etc.) game was exciting.
The students were not on their best behavior.
The test was hard.
The world situation is depressing.
My room is a mess.
My parents are too strict.
School rules are too confining.
It was after midnight, and his parents were out of town.
(For further suggestions, ask your students.)

After you provide the topic sentence, you then can elicit from your students the supporting sentences that use strong verbs, making sure that they do, indeed, support the topic sentence. Then seek the concluding sentence to wrap up the paragraph. Ask students to write a good title for the paragraph and also see if they can insert a good simile somewhere. Make certain that the tense of the verbs remains consistent.

Now that students have written one or two paragraphs as a large group, they are ready to read a few good examples of strong-verb paragraphs. You can show them the ones on the following page. They have been put on a separate page so that you can copy them or put them on overhead transparencies.

> **NOTE:** *The topics are generic enough to be appropriate for all grade levels. The last two were dictated to me, and I wrote them on the overhead for all to see. All main verbs are in bold type. Please note that some are in the past tense and some are in the present tense. Note also that no verbs have been repeated. And, if you are reading these to your students, ask them to add a good simile to each. High-school teachers should demand a few complex sentences.*

Examples of Basic, Elementary Strong-verb Paragraphs

The Happy Girl

Mary *is* happy. She **smiles**. She **laughs** at everything. She **plays** with her toys. Mary *is* very happy today.

My Heart

A heart *is* in my body. It **pumps** my blood. It **runs** my blood around my body. It **makes** a noise thump thump when my doctor listens to it. I *have* a good heart.

The Sad Boy

John *is* sad. He **cries** all the time like a baby. He **frowns**, and he never **smiles**. He **sits** by himself in the corner. John *is* very sad today.

My Sister

My sister *is* a pain. She **takes** stuff out of my room. She **hurts** me by kicking me. She always **comes** in my room when I don't ask her. She **hogs** the t.v. too. That *is* why my big sister is a pain. (She really is not a pain.)

The Funny Dog

The dog *was* very funny. It **chased** its tail round and round, and it never **caught** it. When the funny dog **woofed**, its ears **flopped**. The dog **wagged** its tail so fast it was **like a flag in a big wind**. This dog *was* so funny I bought it.

More Complex Examples of Strong-verb Paragraphs

The Wild Cafeteria

"Prepare yourself," whispered the dean to a teacher, "here come the wild bunch." (Rewrite of boring topic sentence "The students in the cafeteria were wild.") As students got their trays, they **threw** food from table to table. Some **shouted** invectives at the top of their lungs. Soiled trays **littered** the floor where students flung them. Students **stood** on the tables and **danced** to imaginary music. Others **burped** loudly to express their dislike of the school fare. One bold student even **yelled** at the dean, demanding that rock music play during lunch. The dean **croaked** over the loud speaker in a vain attempt to quiet down the students. Food **continued** to splatter on the walls. It **was** a typical lunch in the school cafeteria.

The Messy Room

"Crunch" go my CDs as I walk into my totally messy room! (Rewrite of "My room is a mess.") Clothes **litter** the floor. Sheets and blankets **hang** off the bed in great disarray. Half-empty Coke cans on their side **spill** their contents on the rug. Records **cover** my desk, burying last year's homework. A nasty smell of month-old pizza **wafts** from the overflowing trash can. Moldy school books **peek** out of my packed closet from underneath piles and piles of junk. Food stains from wild food fights **color** the walls. My room is a total disaster, and I **can't leave** it until I clean it up!

4. Clustering for the Paragraphs

Now that your students have written a few paragraphs as a group and have seen some good examples, teach them to cluster for the subjects and strong verbs of the middle sentences so that they can produce paragraphs of their own. You can begin this as a whole-class exercise. Give them several topics and elicit the subject-verb combinations for each of the strong-verb sentences. You can point out here that **it is easier to choose the subject first and then come up with the verb.**

See the cluster below for the example on the previous page about the messy room. Please note the way the students added information to the basic subject/verb of the cluster to make their sentences more interesting. The cluster should be only the basic subject and verb. Sometimes my students prefer to list **all** the subjects first and then come up with the verbs.

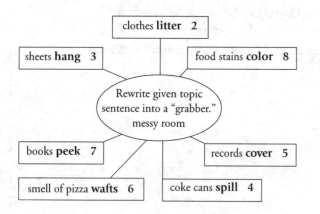

When you have a completed cluster, it is time to decide on the order of your sentences. Students can put numbers by the subject/verb clusters to indicate which should come first, etc., in the paragraph.

5. Writing the Paragraphs

When your students feel comfortable clustering and planning the paragraphs, they are ready to write again, this time in small groups at the elementary- and middle-school levels and as individuals at the high-school level (although if you teach ninth-grade or tenth-grade regular classes, you may find that your students need more group practice).

If you use groups, divide the class into groups of four, give them a topic sentence, and have them write a paragraph together. Repeat this exercise, reducing the number in the groups, until pairs of students are comfortable clustering and writing a paragraph.

It is often very effective to have the groups write their paragraphs on transparencies to share with the class. This adds an air of importance to the exercise. It also lets students participate more in their own learning process.

Finally, most students are ready to write the strong-verb paragraphs on their own. Encourage the use of good vocabulary and transitions ("first," "second," "next," "finally," etc.). Make certain that students have access to dictionaries and thesauruses and a list of the most common transitions. In the lower grades and in compensatory classes, it is a good idea to keep a list of the common transitions on the board until your students get the hang of using these simple devices.

6. Similes, Vocabulary, Sentence Structure

Third grade and higher also may want to require the use of one simile in the paragraph. The use of one or two good similes really raises scores on the state writing assessment test because their use demonstrates a certain sophistication in writing techniques. Encourage the use of compound and complex sentences as well as simple ones that naturally evolve in writing a paragraph. Eighth-grade and higher teachers can even require that a certain number of each type of sentence be used in the paragraph. The scorers of the writing test also are looking for varied sentence structure.

At this point you should also encourage the use of good vocabulary. This, too, raises scores. All grade levels can teach good vocabulary in the context of a story in one of the three Caught'ya books (Kiester, Jane. *Caught'ya! Grammar with a*

Giggle or *Caught'ya Again! More Grammar with a Giggle* or *The Chortling Bard! Grammar with a Giggle for High Schools.* Maupin House, 1990, 1992, and 1998) or any other method that has worked for you. In addition to the vocabulary in the *Caught'yas*, I like to use vocabulary associated with the literature my students are reading.

Again, in the lower grades or in compensatory classes, you may want to post a list of good vocabulary words (perhaps the ones that are in the *Caught'ya* story if you are using that method) somewhere in your classroom, adding words each week to the list.

Strong-verb paragraphs naturally lend themselves to learning some good active verbs as vocabulary words. As students share their paragraphs either by reading them or putting them on the overhead, you might want to post some of their good, active verbs in your room to offer your students more choices as they compose future paragraphs. Invite them to add to the list as they find some "really good verbs" to use. This will drive students to the thesaurus.

I like to require my students to include the following:

- A rewritten topic sentence (change the boring topic sentence to a "grabber")
- Four to six detailed, strong-verb sentences to "show" the meaning of the topic sentence
- At least two "$100" vocabulary words
- A compound sentence
- A complex sentence
- A simile or other literary device
- A concluding sentence that wraps up the paragraph

(See page 17.)

7. Grading the Strong-verb Paragraphs

Once your students begin writing these paragraphs on an individual basis, you are faced with grading them. Never fear! This does not take long. Make it easy on yourself. While you can grade these any way you wish, I suggest that

those of you who teach seventh grade and below (or compensatory classes at any grade level) give three grades: "A" if the paragraph has been written correctly, "B" if there is one mistake, and "C" for more than one error. This encourages care on the part of the students and doesn't eat up too much of your time.

Those of you who teach eighth grade or higher might want to be more exacting in your grading. A copy of the way I grade my eighth graders' strong-verb paragraphs can be found on the next page. I do not recommend that anyone below the eighth-grade level use it unless you have advanced or gifted students who are secure in their writing egos, as the grades on the paragraphs initially tend to be rather low until students learn the craft. I make copies of the sheet and give it to each of my students so that they can refer to it as they compose their paragraphs. **(See page 18.)**

8. An Eye-opening Activity and a Conclusion to the Strong Verbs

I cannot stress how much difference the use of strong, action verbs makes in a student's writing. I suggest holding frequent "strong-verb reality checks" with your students. This also makes the point with them that something needs to change. Get some large, bright markers, instruct your students to get out any piece of writing that they have recently completed, assign groups, and you are ready to begin the simple exercise.

Within their groups, students should pour over all writing samples (one for each student), looking for the "dead verbs." They must mark each "dead verb" with a big **X** over it. Instruct the groups to be thorough and recheck each paper at least twice. If you don't already have a bulletin board with the "dead verbs" posted on it, you might want to put them on the board for reference.

When students have finished marking the papers, have them hold up the results. Students are shocked (especially before writing strong-verb paragraphs) at how often they use the "helping verbs" and how little they use strong, active ones. This simple activity makes a big difference in my students' attitudes towards writing the often difficult strong-verb paragraphs and in really making an effort to use more active verbs in their writing in general.

If you look at literature, you will find that the use of strong, active verbs abounds. This is one of the hallmarks of literature and of good writing in general. When the people who score the state writing test in your state score the papers, they probably don't even consciously notice the use of active verbs, but I know that my students who are able to use these verbs consistently, are the ones who earn the highest scores. The use of strong, active verbs really does make a difference!

To aid students, I put up the following on an overhead. This not only helps them to cluster, but it also reminds them of the paragraph requirements.

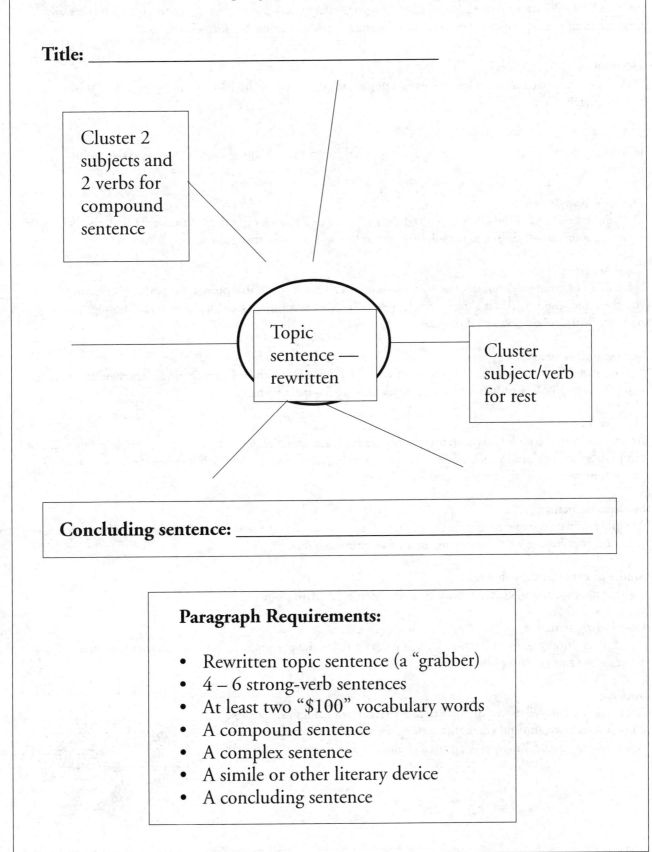

Title: _____

Cluster 2 subjects and 2 verbs for compound sentence

Topic sentence — rewritten

Cluster subject/verb for rest

Concluding sentence: _____

Paragraph Requirements:

- Rewritten topic sentence (a "grabber)
- 4 – 6 strong-verb sentences
- At least two "$100" vocabulary words
- A compound sentence
- A complex sentence
- A simile or other literary device
- A concluding sentence

FYI — How Your Teacher Scores the SVP

NOTE: Extra Points +5 if it is typed. **+2** for each vocabulary word correctly used (**up to 10**). **+5** if it is really original, exceptionally well written, especially amusing, or otherwise distinguishes itself.

Heading

Is the heading correct? You can lose the usual **ten points** off the top of the 100 for the assignment if it is not. Do not be careless here.

Title

Is it different from the topic sentence? Are there capital letters in the right places? You can lose **five points** for this.

Plan and Rough draft

Did you somehow plan the strong verbs and their subjects in a cluster, outline, or whatever? Have you included the corrected rough draft? Failure to include any part of this will cost you **five points**.

Topic sentence

Is it a complete sentence, and is it really a topic sentence? This is worth **five points**. Since the teacher usually gives you the topic sentence, this is a freebie grade. Be careful. I like to ask my students to turn the "boring" topic sentence into a good "grabber" if they can.

Strong-verb sentences

In the six middle sentences, are only the main verbs highlighted? Are they all strong verbs? Are they all different? You will lose up to **five points** for incorrectly identifying the main verbs.

Dead verbs

Are there any in the middle six sentences? Except in the topic sentence and the concluding sentence, you will lose **ten points for each** dead verb used, for each strong verb that is repeated, for each fragment up to a total of 60 points, one for each of the six sentences!

Sentence structure

Are the required type of sentences included? Do all the sentences make sense? Are all the sentences complete sentences (not fragments)? You can lose up to **five points** for this.

Simile or other literary device

Is there an original simile? Has it been circled? This is worth **five points**.

Concluding sentence

Is it different from the first sentence? Does it wrap up the entire paragraph or is it just another sentence. You can lose another **five points** here.

Spelling

Are there any misspelled words? You will lose *five points each* up to a possible 25 points so be careful and check! Misspelling more than one word can earn you a negative grade! Be smart. Consult a dictionary or a parent.

STEP TWO

Teach Students How to Score the State Writing Assessment Test

1. Teaching Yourself How to Score the Essays Holistically

Before you can teach your students how to score the essays required for the test, you yourself must be comfortable in your own ability to score. This is not easy in a room by yourself. Many school districts offer workshops in holistic scoring. If your district offers one, take it. If it does not, try what I suggest below.

> **NOTE:** *If you are a new teacher (or, like me, did not major in English in college) and are not already familiar with the format of a basic essay or a short narrative, this would be a good time to turn to Step Three and read the first section to give yourself an overview.*

You can give yourself a one-teacher workshop practice in scoring the essays by copying the examples of last year's test (if your state prints them up for you), taking off the scores, mixing them up, and practicing scoring them yourself. (Try not to look at the answers as you copy the examples!) After you assign a score to each essay or narrative, check with the official answer. Like the teachers who attend my workshops, if you do this for 53 essays, you soon will feel quite at home assigning scores to essays and stories.

In my workshops, the teachers work as a large group and then in small groups before they score the tests individually. And while, initially, you probably will make more mistakes than you would if you were working in a group, I predict that you will achieve the end result — feeling comfortable about scoring the essays. You then can use these same examples to train your students.

If your state does not print out examples of each year's test results, use the examples in the last section of this book, **Fifty-three Examples for Scoring Practice**, and trust your instincts as a teacher who has graded many papers in the course of your career. Remember that when you score holistically, you are only looking for the basics, an impression. You are not reading carefully and analyzing. This section of the book also will help you learn how to score the papers. Read on.

2. Obtaining Your Examples and Teaching the Basic Criteria of Scoring

Before students are taught the elements of a basic essay or narrative, they should be taught how to score one. By seeing examples of good, mediocre, and bad essays and learning to score them, students become aware of what constitutes a good paper. Only after students have read quite a few samples, analyzed, and scored them, are they ready to learn and apply to their own writing the actual components of the basic essay or narrative. **So, where do you get the examples?**

- You need the examples from the booklet your state (hopefully) publishes each year on the results of the previous year's writing test. The State of Florida publishes the yearly booklet, "Florida Writes." In this booklet are examples of actual test essays that received each of the scores on the six-point rubric (to be explained later in this **Step**). That is a total of fourteen essays, one for each of the seven possible scores for each of the two topics. Other states send back student papers that have been scored. With names removed, the good ones could be used as examples.
- Although I teach eighth grade, I use examples from both fourth-, eighth-, and tenth-grade tests as practice for teaching my students how to score. Copy the examples from your state's booklets of the past few years, putting a piece of paper over the scores before you copy them so that the students can score these with no possibility of peeking at the actual answers. Run off class sets of each. It is also helpful to number each paper for identification purposes. Since you can use these year after year, it is a good investment of time and paper.
- Another way to obtain examples is to use ones that your previous years' students have written to practice for the test. The only disadvantage to using these is that they were not officially scored. Find a willing parent with a computer who can type the papers as is, mistakes and all. You then can make overhead transparencies or copies for your students to practice grading.
- You also can use the anonymous samples written by fourth, seventh, eighth, and tenth graders that are included in the last section of this book, **Fifty-three Examples for Scoring Practice**. (In fact,

I have used these with my students for several years now.) Please note that a few of these examples have been slightly changed by additions or deletions so that they fit more precisely the score being illustrated. (Scores of **6** and zero are very hard to come by.)

An analysis of the score follows each paper. Try not to look at the scores before reading them yourself. You can then use them for scoring practice for yourself and for your students. Since these were not the actual papers of the test (although one set is the same subject as this year's fourth-grade topic) and hence were not officially scored, they were scored by me and by the teachers who kindly let me use them in this book. I think, however, that the scores reflect fairly accurately what the papers would receive officially.

Before you pass out the examples to grade, however, you need to teach your students the basic criteria for scoring. A précis of this follows on a separate page to facilitate showing it to your students. These are the official criteria for the State of Florida, sent to my district by the Department of Education in Tallahassee, Florida. Almost all other states use the same or very similar criteria.

The Florida criteria for scoring are quite simple: focus, organization, supporting ideas, and conventions. A definition of each follows on **page 22**. You might want to teach these to your students just for their own knowledge. Obviously, you will have to simplify the definitions if you teach elementary school.

If you do not teach in Florida, or your state does not use a six-point rubric, get a copy of the official scoring criteria from your English supervisor. If you cannot obtain a copy of your state's criteria, use the Florida one as it probably does not differ too much from your state's criteria. The Six-point Modified Holistic Rubric on the last page of this Step also comes from the Florida Department of Education. It, too, may differ slightly from the rubric that your state uses; however, if you cannot obtain a copy of your state's

scoring rubric, Florida's will suffice since most states score fairly similarly.

3. The Grading Rubric and Lesson Plans to Teach it to Your Students

While the actual test is scored on a four, five, or six-point modified holistic rubrick, depending on your state, (see the sample six-point draft on **page 25**), at first, you will want to teach your students how to score more simply. Begin with teaching them a High, Medium, Low method of scoring using the form on **page 24**. You can use this to make copies for your students to use as they practice. Sometimes I put four on a page. I have printed it three times on **page 24** as I assume that your paper and copying situation is probably as desperate as mine.

Once students understand the four components of a good essay or narrative, it should be easy to teach them to grade on a three-point scale for each component. If you think of High as **5** or **6**, Medium as **3** or **4**, and Low as **1** or **2**, then those of you who teach middle or high school can gradually move your students to the six-point rubric after they are comfortable with the high, medium, and low scoring. My eighth graders prefer having more options and actually get quite good at scoring accurately on the six-point rubric! They even become adept at spotting **zero** essays that are well written but off the topic.

> **NOTE:** *This is actually a seven-point rubric since zero counts as a score. A zero is reserved for blank papers, essays that are illegible, or essays that are so far off the topic that they bear no resemblance to it.*

On **page 23**, I offer you some practical lesson plans to teach your students how to score the essays or narratives. These plans take at least five days to teach effectively. The more practice your students have scoring the essays, the better they will understand how to write them. The better they understand how to write them, the higher their scores will be.

The Basic Criteria for Scoring the State Writing Assessment Test

Focus

Clarity with which the paper presents and maintains a clear main idea, point of view, theme, or unifying event; consistent awareness of the topic; exclusion of extraneous information.

Organization

Structure or plan of development (beginning, middle, and end); logical relationship of ideas; use of paragraphing and transitional devices.

Supporting Ideas

Quality of detail or support; examples or reasons clearly related to specific context; word choice, specificity, depth, accuracy or credibility, and thoroughness.

Conventions

Mechanics of punctuation, capitalization, spelling, and word usage; sentence structure.

Lesson Plans for Practicing Scoring

Beforehand

1. Run off many copies of the Focused Analytical Scoring Sheet on the following page.

2. Make overhead copies of at least two examples of essays (and narratives if your grade level in your state tests that type of writing) for each score.

3. Run off class sets of many examples of actual test essays. Be sure to include at least three examples of each score from **0** to **the top score in your state.**

4. Make sure that you divide your class into heterogeneous response groups of three and four.

Lesson

1. Teach the four components of a good essay. **(See previous pages.)**

2. Teach the scale of scoring — high, medium, low. **(See next page.)**

3. Show at least two examples of each score on the overhead. Have students read them and, as a class, score them on one of the scoring sheets that follow this page.

4. Divide students into groups of four. Pass out copies of three more papers, one high, one medium, and one low. Ask each group to read the papers and score them on another score sheet. Do this several times until students are comfortable with scoring on their own. After each session, debrief the students by discussing and analyzing why each example deserved its score.

5. Do the same with more examples, either copied (one set per student) or on an overhead transparency, but this time have students grade them individually. You can get examples from your state's booklet, from the examples in the last section of this book, or from teachers who saved practice papers from last year. Middle- and high-school teachers can gradually move to using the six-point rubric as their students grow more comfortable with scoring.

6. Now students are ready for the next step, **Step Three.**

Focused Analytical Scoring

FOCUS _____ High _____ Medium _____ Low
    ON THE TOPIC?
    NO UNRELATED INFORMATION?   RESTATE TOPIC OR
                                         KEY WORDS EACH PARAGRAPH

ORGANIZATION _____ High _____ Medium _____ Low
    BEGINNING, MIDDLE, END?
    PATTERN OF ORGANIZATION?   TRANSITIONS?
                                         APPROPRIATE SIMILE USE?

SUPPORT _____ High _____ Medium _____ Low
    EXPANDED MAIN IDEA(S)?
    NITTY GRITTY DETAILS, EXAMPLES?   PIZZAZZ?
    SPECIFIC LANGUAGE (GOOD VOCABULARY)?   TOPIC AND END SENTENCES

CONVENTIONS _____ High _____ Medium _____ Low
    SPELLING?
    CAPITALIZATION?
    PUNCTUATION?
    USAGE?

                      SCORE: HIGH   MEDIUM   LOW

Focused Analytical Scoring

FOCUS _____ High _____ Medium _____ Low
    ON THE TOPIC?
    NO UNRELATED INFORMATION?   RESTATE TOPIC OR
                                         KEY WORDS EACH PARAGRAPH

ORGANIZATION _____ High _____ Medium _____ Low
    BEGINNING, MIDDLE, END?
    PATTERN OF ORGANIZATION?   TRANSITIONS?
                                         APPROPRIATE SIMILE USE?

SUPPORT _____ High _____ Medium _____ Low
    EXPANDED MAIN IDEA(S)?
    NITTY GRITTY DETAILS, EXAMPLES?   PIZZAZZ?
    SPECIFIC LANGUAGE (GOOD VOCABULARY)?   TOPIC AND END SENTENCES

CONVENTIONS _____ High _____ Medium _____ Low
    SPELLING?
    CAPITALIZATION?
    PUNCTUATION?
    USAGE?

                      SCORE: HIGH   MEDIUM   LOW

Focused Analytical Scoring

FOCUS _____ High _____ Medium _____ Low
    ON THE TOPIC?
    NO UNRELATED INFORMATION?   RESTATE TOPIC OR
                                         KEY WORDS EACH PARAGRAPH

ORGANIZATION _____ High _____ Medium _____ Low
    BEGINNING, MIDDLE, END?
    PATTERN OF ORGANIZATION?   TRANSITIONS?
                                         APPROPRIATE SIMILE USE?

SUPPORT _____ High _____ Medium _____ Low
    EXPANDED MAIN IDEA(S)?
    NITTY GRITTY DETAILS, EXAMPLES?   PIZZAZZ?
    SPECIFIC LANGUAGE (GOOD VOCABULARY)?   TOPIC AND END SENTENCES

CONVENTIONS _____ High _____ Medium _____ Low
    SPELLING?
    CAPITALIZATION?
    PUNCTUATION?
    USAGE?

                      SCORE: HIGH   MEDIUM   LOW

Six-Point Modified Holistic Rubric

0 Points

Either the student did not write at all, the writing is totally illegible, or the writing is totally off the topic.

1 Point

The writing may be only slightly related to the topic. Fragmentary or incoherent listing of related ideas and/or sentences may occur. Little, if any, development of support and/or organizational pattern is apparent. Limited or inappropriate vocabulary frequently obscures meaning. Gross errors in sentence structure and usage may impede communication. Frequent and blatant errors may occur in the basic conventions of mechanics and usage, and commonly used words are misspelled.

2 Points

The writing is related to the topic but offers little support. Little evidence of an organizational pattern may be demonstrated. Development of details may be erratic, inadequate, or illogical. Vocabulary is limited, inappropriate, or vague. Gross errors in sentence structure may occur. Errors in basic conventions of mechanics and usage may occur and commonly used words may be misspelled.

3 Points

The writing demonstrates an awareness of the topic but may include extraneous or loosely related material. The paper may lack a sense of completeness or wholeness. Some support is included but may not be developed. An organizational pattern has been attempted. Vocabulary is adequate but may be limited, predictable, or occasionally vague. Most sentences are complete. Knowledge of the conventions of mechanics and usage is usually demonstrated and commonly used words are usually spelled correctly.

4 Points

The writing is generally related to the topic with adequate support, although development may be uneven. The paper exhibits some sense of completeness or wholeness. Logical order is apparent, although some lapses may occur. Word choice is adequate. Most sentences are complete. The paper generally follows the conventions of mechanics, usage, and spelling.

5 Points

The writing focuses on the topic with ample support and has a logical structure. The paper conveys a sense of completeness and wholeness. The writing demonstrates a mature command of language, including precision in word choice and variation in sentence structure. With rare exceptions, sentences are complete except when fragments are used purposefully. The paper generally follows the conventions of mechanics, usage, and spelling.

6 Points

The writing is focused, purposeful, and reflects insight into the writing situation. The paper conveys a sense of completeness and wholeness with adherence to the main idea and a logical progression of ideas. The support is substantial, specific, relevant, concrete, and/or illustrative. The paper demonstrates a commitment to and an involvement with the subject, clarity in presentation of ideas, and may use creative writing strategies appropriate to the purpose of the paper. The writing demonstrates a mature command of language with freshness of expression. Sentences are complete except when fragments are purposefully used. Few, if any, conventional errors occur.

(From the Florida Department of Education, changed for clarity here)

4. Helpful Things to Point Out as Your Students Practice Scoring

As you read and discuss with your students the good examples of writing that received the highest scores, there are some things you might want to point out. As my students are learning to score, I always read at least one good example a day to subliminally drill into their heads what constitutes a good essay or story. I point out the following:

- Good grabbers that catch our attention such as conversations, the use of onomatopoeia or a question, or beginning with a quotation (correctly punctuated, of course).
- Restating the topic in the first paragraph and referring to it in all subsequent paragraphs.
- The use of any literary device.
- Strong-verb use, especially in descriptions.
- The use of a topic sentence and a concluding sentence in each of the four to five paragraphs.
- Indenting paragraphs as well as correctly punctuated quotes, compound, and complex sentences. Please note that Caught'yas (Kiester, 1990, 1993, 1998, 2000-see **Bibliography**) teach these grammar and mechanical skills more effectively.
- Any "$100, big, juicy" vocabulary word that is used in the paper.
- A strong conclusion that wraps up the essay or story.
- A theme that threads itself through the paper (such as a reference to a bird or something as a simple metaphor).
- And, most importantly, the use of nitty-gritty detail. I point out every use and non-use of it. When a general statement is made and not followed up with detail, I ask my students to supply that detail. For example, the statement, "I hate my sister because she messes in my room" is not considered nitty-gritty detail; but to say, "I hate my sister because she messes in my room and plays my CDs, takes my stuffed animals off the bed, tries on my clothes, and sneaks a peek in my diary," is nitty-gritty detail. The more examples you read to your students (especially the younger ones) the better chance you will have that they will learn to elaborate in their writing.

STEP THREE

Teach Students How to Plan and Write a Standard Five-paragraph Essay (and Narrative Story) and Have Students Plan, Write, Evaluate, and Score at Least Fifteen before the Day of the Test

1. Introduction

Step Three is a little more complicated than the other three **Steps** since it involves so much material on two different genres - essays and fictional stories. You might want to read through the entire chapter and use the sections that are appropriate and/or useful for your students.

I think you will find the nine sections self-explanatory and will be able to use them with your students without much difficulty. Please note that all these ideas have been classroom tested again and again with my students and also by other teachers. You may use a few or all of them, depending on the level and the needs of your students. Some parts of a section, like the **Useful Devices**, you may want to copy and give to your students as reference. Some sections, like **# 5, Learning to Produce Nitty-gritty Details in the Middle**, contain activities to use with your classes. And, still other sections, # 7, **Procedure for Practicing the Actual Writing** for example, include lesson plans to help you organize.

The last section, **210 Practice Prompts** is simply a list of thirty prompts/topics of each type that is used. Your students may be required to produce only two or all of them, depending on grade level and your state's requirements. Pick and choose the ones you think best exemplify the topics your state will use on the actual test. In fact, some of the topics were actual prompts on previous tests in several states.

2. Teaching Students the Definition of What They Will Write

Before teaching students how to write the standard essay (or story) for a good score on the state writing assessment test, you need to first teach them what comprises a good, standard essay or story. Most teachers call the topic or "starter" for an essay or story a "prompt." Students also need to understand that a standard four- to six-paragraph essay is the type they will have to write for the state test if asked to produce an expository/clarification or persuasive paper.

A standard essay can be expository/clarification, descriptive, or persuasive. A story is narrative. If your state, asks for a short narrative or an expository/clarification essay of fourth graders, and you teach fourth grade or below, you will want to stress the differences between a narrative story and an expository/clarification, descriptive, essay and teach your students to recognize the difference. This is imperative since clustering for narratives and essays is different, and one of the dangers elementary-age children face on the writing assessment is writing an expository/clarification essay instead of a story for a narrative topic.

Those of you who teach fifth grade or above in most states need to prepare your students to write an expository/clarification, descriptive, or persuasive essay and make sure that your students know the difference between the two. One of the dangers seventh or eighth and tenth graders face on the writing assessment is treating a persuasive essay as an expository/clarification one (explaining the topic rather than arguing a side of it). Both middle- and high-school students have trouble with this. The difference between expository/clarification and persuasive essays is not as clear as between expository/clarification essays and narrative stories.

There are three tricks that other teachers and I have found useful to teach students the difference among the four types of writing they may be expected to produce on the state writing assessment test. The first two tricks are simple and require very little preparation on your part although students enjoy the second trick more. The third is more complicated, but it is worth the trouble because after students master the concept, it can be an extremely effective literary tool. And, after you and your students practice **Trick #3** a bit, it also can become a spontaneous, thirty-second activity every time you read anything in class as a part of any assignment.

❤ Trick #1 - Identify Types of Writing as You and Your Students Score Essays and Narratives in Step Two of This Book

As you score the essays in **Step Two** of this book, you also can ask your students to identify the type of essay they are reading-descriptive, expository/clarification, narrative, or persuasive/point-of-view-as well as to score each essay. In the same vein, using the examples in the last section of this book, pick one from each type of writing. (The score does not matter as long as it is identifiable as one of the types of writing.) Read these four examples to your students and ask them to identify the type of writing.

This activity can be done for an entire class period as you pick essays at random from the back of the book, or it can be used as a mini-lesson at the beginning of the day or period as you read only a few randomly chosen essays or stories for the class to identify.

❤ Trick #2 - The Hat Trick

The second trick involves a hat (or a small box), a copy of the prompts listed in the last section of this chapter, a pair of scissors, and two minutes a day for practice. First, copy from at the end of this chapter the prompts that pertain to your students. For example, my eighth graders are tested only on expository and persuasive essays, so I would copy all of those prompts and throw in only a few of the descriptive and narrative ones just to add a level of difficulty.

Then, cut out all the prompts, fold them up, and place them in the hat (or box). Daily, after the *Caught'ya* or at the beginning of the period, ask a student to draw a topic from the hat. Ask the student to read the prompt out loud. Ask the class to identify the type of prompt and the key words that helped them in their identification:

Descriptive-describe;
Expository/Clarification-explain, clarify;
Narrative-tell, story, (a recount of what happened);
Persuasive/Point of View-persuade, convince.

Although you probably should do no more than two or three of prompts a day (to keep the activity interesting), it is a good idea to do this activity at least three times a week for several months.

♥ Trick #3 — Read Brief Passages to Learn to Identify the Four Different Types of Writing Required on Tests.

This activity is effective with any piece of reading material you happen to be using in your classroom. To give you examples, I pulled four books from my shelves, perused them briefly, and came up with the following passages. When I picked the passage in *Harry Potter*, I deliberately had not yet read the book so that I could illustrate how easy it is to find a passage in a book for the purpose of this exercise.

First, pick a book, preferably the one your students are currently reading or one, like *Harry Potter* that is very popular with your students. Then skim the book yourself and find brief examples of the four types of writing-descriptive, expository, narrative, persuasive. This may sound difficult, but, once you begin doing this, you can't stop!

Next, type up these examples following the examples I give you below. Identify the book and the title of the book, the author, and the page number to keep it legal. Run off a class set of these examples. Now you are ready to begin the activity with your students.

Pass out copies of the passages and first, as an entire class, identify the type of writing in each passage. To make it easier for students, it is a good idea to group one example of each type as I have done below. When students are comfortable identifying the four different types of writing, give them another set of examples, divide the class into groups (making sure that each student has a "job" like reader, runner, leader—to keep group on task—, and recorder), and ask each group to identify the types of writing. The recorder records the answers. When the groups have completed the exercise, discuss the answers as a class. The next step is to ask students to do the same on their own, without the help of their peers.

After students become adept at recognizing the types of writing, this activity can be contin-ued all year for reinforcement. You can do this orally without any advance preparation. Simply identify passages as students read. This can become a game with your students-see how many examples of the four types of writing you can find in a given chapter.

Listed below are sample passages from four books. After the passages, I have included a key to help you since the line between persuasive and expository is sometimes thin. If you disagree with me, you may be right. After all, the powers-that-be who decide on the topics for the Florida test, in my and many other teachers' opinions once chose an expository topic for the fourth grade and called it a narrative.

From *Winnie the Pooh* by A. A. Milne

A) Once upon a time, a very long time ago now, about last Friday, Winnie-the-Pooh lived in a forest all by himself under the name of Sanders.

One day when he was out walking, he came to an open place in the middle of the forest, and in the middle of this place was a large oak-tree, and, from the top of the tree, there came a loud buzzing noise.

Winnie-the-Pooh sat down at the foot of the tree, put his head between his paws and began to think. (pp. 2-3)

B) "I have just seen Eeyore," he began, "and poor Eeyore is in a Very Sad Condition because it's his birthday, and nobody has taken any notice of it, and he's very Gloomy-you know what Eeyore is - and there he was, and..." (p. 76)

C) Little soft clouds played happily in a blue sky, skipping from time to time in front of the sun as if they had come to put it out, and then sliding away suddenly so that the next might have his turn. Through them and between them the sun shone bravely; and a copse which had worn its firs all the year round seemed old and dowdy now beside the new green lace which the beeches had put on so prettily. (p. 45)

D) PLAN TO CAPTURE BABY ROO
1. General Remarks. Kanga runs faster than any of Us, even Me.

2. More General Remarks. Kanga never takes her eye off Baby Roo, except when he's safely buttoned up in her pocket.

3. Therefore. If we are to capture Baby Roo, we must get a Long Start, because Kanga runs faster than any of Us, even Me.

8. Another Thought But, if Pooh was talking to her very excitedly, she might look the other way for a moment.

9. And then I could run away with Roo. (p. 93-94)

From *Charlotte's Web* by E. B. White

A) Twilight settled over Zuckerman's barn, and a feeling of peace. Swallows passed on silent wings, in and out of the doorways, bringing food to their young ones. From across the road a bird sang, "Whippoorwill, whippoorwill!" (p. 62)

B) Life in the barn was very good-night and day, winter and summer, spring and fall, dull days and bright days. It was the best place to be, thought Wilbur, this warm delicious cellar, with the garrulous geese, the changing seasons, the heat of the sun, the passage of swallows, the nearness of rats, the sameness of sheep, the love of spiders, the smell of manure, and the glory of everything. (p. 183)

C) "It was a never-to-be-forgotten battle," said Charlotte. "There was the fish, caught only by one fin, and its tail wildly thrashing and shining in the sun. There was the web, sagging dangerously under the weight of the fish. ...There was my cousin, slipping in, dodging out, beaten mercilessly over the head by the wildly thrashing fish, dancing in, dancing out, throwing her threads out, fighting hard. First she threw a left around the tail. The fish lashed back... " (p. 103)

D) "It's cruel," replied Wilbur, who did not intend to be argued out of his position.

"Well, you can't talk," said Charlotte. "You have your meals brought to you in a pail. Nobody feeds me. I have to get my own living. I live by my wits. I have to be sharp and clever, lest I go hungry. I have to think things out, catch what I can, take what comes. And it just so happens, my friend, that what comes is flies and insects and bugs. And furthermore," said Charlotte, shaking one of her legs, "do you realize that if I didn't catch bugs and eat them, bugs would increase and multiply and get so numerous that they'd destroy the earth, wipe out everything?" (p. 40)

From *I Know Why the Caged Bird Sings* by Maya Angelou

A) The missionary ladies of the Christian Methodist Episcopal Church helped Momma prepare the pork for sausage. They squeezed their fat arms elbow deep in the ground meat, mixed it with gray nose-opening sage, pepper, and salt, and made tasty little samples for all obedient children who brought wood for the slick black stove. (p. 19)

B) Later Mother made a broth and sat on the edge of the bed to feed me. The liquid went down my throat like bones. My belly and behind were as heavy as cold iron, but it seemed my head had gone away and pure air had replaced it on my shoulders, Bailey read to me from *The Rover Boys* until he got sleepy and went to bed. (p. 67)

C) Momma said, "Dentist Lincoln. It's my grandbaby here. She got two rotten teeth that's giving her a fit. ... She had this toothache purt' near four days now, and today I said, 'Young lady, you going to the Dentist.'" ...

"I know, Dentist Lincoln. But, this here is just my little grandbaby, and she ain't gone be no trouble to you... Seem like to me, Dentist Lincoln, you might look after her. She ain't nothing but a little mite. And seems like maybe you owe me a favor or two... I wouldn't press on you like this for myself but I can't take No. Not for my grandbaby. When you come to borrow my money you didn't have to beg. You asked me, and I lent it." (p. 160)

D) The wind blew over the roof and ruffled the shingles. It whistled sharply under the closed door. The chimney made fearful sounds of protest as it was invaded by the urgent gusts. (p.128)

From *Harry Potter and the Sorcerer's Stone* by J. K. Rowling

A) He brought Harry a hamburger and they sat down on plastic seats to eat them. Harry kept looking around. Everything looked so strange, somehow. (p. 86)

B) "Everyone things I'm special," he said at last. "all those people in the Leaky Cauldron.... But I don't know anything about magic at all. How can they expect great things? I'm famous and I can't even remember what I'm famous for. I don't know what happened when Vol-, sorry-I mean, the night my parents died." (p. 86)

C) Harry had never imagined such a strange and splendid place. It was lit by thousands and thousands of candles that were floating in midair over four long tables where the rest of the students were sitting. These tables were laid with glittering golden plates and goblets. At the top of the hall was another long table where the teachers were sitting... (p. 116)

D) "*This*," said Wood, "is the Golden Snitch, and it's the most important ball of the lot. It's very hard to catch because it's so fast and difficult to see. It's the Seeker's job to catch it. You've got to weave in and out of the Chasers, Beaters, Bludgers, and Quaffle to get it before the other team's Seeker, because whichever Seeker catches the Snitch wins his team an extra hundred and fifty points, so they nearly always win.... A game of Quidditch only ends when the Snitch is caught, so it can go on for ages... (p. 169)

Key to Above Passages:

Winnie the Pooh
A) Narrative
B) Persuasive/Point-of View
C) Descriptive
D) Expository/Clarification

Charlotte's Web
A) Descriptive
B) Expository/Clarification
C) Narrative
D) Persuasive/Point-of-View

I Know Why the Caged Bird Sings
A) Expository/Clarification
B) Narrative
C) Persuasive/Point-of-View
D) Descriptive

Harry Potter and the Sorcerer's Stone
A) Narrative
B) Persuasive/Point-of-View
C) Descriptive
D) Expository/Clarification

Narrative Story

A narrative story tells a story based on a real or imaginary event or recounts a personal or fictional experience. It should include specific detail to liven up the story. It requires a beginning, a middle, and an end of some kind that wraps up the story. Dialogue is a good idea, and the narrative should be less structured than the essays. **The idea is to tell a coherent story in chronological order that is interesting, provides good detail and description, clearly expresses the writer's voice, is imaginative, and does not contain extraneous side stories.** It is not an essay, and therefore paragraphing is not as important.

Expository/Clarification Essay

An expository/clarification essay instructs, gives information, or explains something, as, for instance, "Why one particular year was your best school year." It also can clarify a process such as making school rules or defining a concept like "beauty." The support in the middle of this essay should provide specific, nitty-gritty examples or relate an incident to further clarify or explain the topic without straying from the topic. **The author is explaining, not arguing or taking a side.**

Persuasive/Point of View Essay

A persuasive essay tries to persuade the reader of something; for example, "Should the school year be extended by ten days?" The specific details necessary in the middle of this essay must support the writer's point of view or argument. **In a persuasive essay, the writer needs to come up with some good evidence in the form of examples or detailed reasons to make his/her point, being careful not to stray from the argument at hand.** The writer needs to constantly keep in mind that he/she is **not** explaining the topic.

Descriptive Essay

The descriptive essay varies from state to state. Some states encourage the use of all five senses to enhance the description. Most states, however, require a visual description from three focal points of the object or place to be described. In other words, the writer should describe the object or place from three different angles or focal points. This should be done so vividly that the reader clearly can picture the object/place being described. Other senses may be used and can even be the focal point of a paragraph (sound, for example) to enhance the visual, but the **visual image must be maintained throughout**, or the score will fall.

Students may be directed to describe such things as a kitchen, a place where many people gather, a storm, or any object or place common to all children, but usually not a person. Each of the three supporting paragraphs in the middle of the essay should be vivid, strong-verb descriptions of one focal point of the object or place. For example, to describe a season such as fall, a student might take the different focal points of the trees, the leaves, the ground, the weather, the sounds of fall (keeping the visual in mind), or the overall panorama. To describe an object, the writer might want to describe the front, the back, and then the sides, or instead tackle the appearance, the colors, and the shape of the object. In other words, divide the place or object to be described into three focal points.

In a state that encourages more use of senses in addition to vision, that same description of the fall scene, for example, could have each of the three supportive/descriptive middle para-graphs showing what fall looks like, what it feels like (weather, etc.), and what it smells like (wet leaves, and so on). A writer really could get into fall sounds in the woods, the swishing of leaves under feet, and the stillness of cold weather.

In any descriptive essay, the author is describing, not telling a story or explaining something. The descriptive essay is a dangerous type of required writing since it is so easy to turn it into a narrative story.

There are four key things to remember in writing a descriptive essay.

- Take three focal points of the object or place and **describe** each one in one of the middle paragraphs;
- Use strong, active verbs;
- Keep the essay in the third person (avoid use of "I"); and
- Never use the words "reason" or "because" since then you would be clarifying or explaining rather than describing.

In general, the expository/clarification and persuasive essays take **one** point of view and expand on it. The narrative tells **one** story. The descriptive essay describes **one** object or place. Neither the essays nor the narrative should jump from topic to topic or switch from one genre to another. On the following five pages I have given you the basic elements of essays and a narrative in a form that you can use with your students.

Basic Expository/Clarification, Descriptive, or Persuasive/Point of View Essay

A basic essay has about five paragraphs. The number does not have to be exact, but at least four paragraphs are usually necessary for an effective essay. As you write your essays, no matter whether descriptive, expository/clarification, or persuasive, you should keep in mind that it is extremely important to do the following:

- Keep to the topic at hand. Do not stray or go off on a tangent. Do not turn a persuasive or descriptive essay into an expository/clarification one or vice versa.

- Use great vocabulary. You want to show that you have a good command of words that is above and beyond what the average student your age knows.

- Organize yourself well. Never make a statement that you do not back up or support. Develop that support well.

- Use a good quote, even if you make it up.

- Use transitions such as first, second, third, next, before or after, and finally. (See list of transitions)

- Do not be afraid to argue or develop a side of a topic with which you disagree. Do not be afraid to make up something. You will probably dislike the topic given to you on the actual test. It is important to learn to **quickly** cluster several ideas to see which one you can substantiate with good support or detail, from which you can compose a good essay. Sometimes in a persuasive essay you may find that the point of view you can easily support with convincing arguments will be the point of view with which you disagree. Go for it. Be a "devil's advocate." On the actual test, you will be evaluated not on what your opinion is but how well and how passionately you support the stand that you take.

The Five Paragraphs of a Basic Essay

It is important to learn the components of each paragraph in the standard essay. Here is a précis. Note that these components follow, in paragraph form instead of sentence form, the same pattern as the strong-verb paragraphs.

Expository/Clarification, Descriptive, or Persuasive

Paragraph #1 —

- This is your introduction. Begin with a good "grabber."
- Restate the topic and define it.
- State three arguments (persuasive), explanations (expository/clarification), examples, or focal points to describe (descriptive).
- Conclude with a transition sentence that leads into the next paragraph.

Paragraph #2, Paragraph #3, and Paragraph #4 —

- These paragraphs are the body of your essay.
- Use a transition at the beginning of each paragraph. Try to be different.
- In each paragraph you develop **one** of your arguments, points, focal points of description, or explanations as fully as you can, restating the argument (persuasive), explanation (expository/clarification) or object of description (descriptive) and then expanding on it with examples or evidence that support it.
- These are the most important paragraphs in the grading of the State Assessment Test. The judges are looking at how you support the broad statements you make. Use nitty-gritty **detail**!
- Each of these paragraphs (as well as the body of the essay) needs an introductory sentence and a concluding sentence.
- These are the paragraphs where it is important to use spectacular vocabulary to show a good knowledge of words.
- A little well-placed humor and creativity definitely add to the quality of the paper.

Paragraph #5 —

- This is your conclusion.
- Restate your topic in words that are different from those in paragraph 1.
- Summarize paragraphs 2, 3, and 4.
- Draw a one-sentence conclusion.
- End with a "zinger" that makes the reader think or smile.

Basic Short Narrative

A basic narrative (or story) must contain a definite beginning, middle, and end. Paragraphing isn't as important as chronological order of events in the story. The narrative format is based on telling a story in a logical order. A story needs to be told with passion and a clear progression from beginning to end. Dialogue and details add to the quality of the story as do descriptions of the scene. Remember the following as you write your narrative.

- Keep to the story you are telling. Do not stray or go off on a tangent. Do not tell a story within a story.

- Make sure that the events in your story happen in a chronological order. Do not skip around in your telling of the story or jump from one event to another or suddenly change scene.

- Use great vocabulary. You want to show that you have a good command of words that are above and beyond those the average student your age knows.

- Use dialogue or other creative writing strategies somewhere in your story.

- Use similes and strong verbs to enhance descriptions.

- Make sure that you include enough detail to make your story interesting to the reader, to keep him/her hooked.

- Write with a clear voice. Pick whether you want to write using "I" or a third person (he or she) and stick with it.

The Beginning, Middle, and End of a Narrative

Beginning

- Begin with a "grabber" to hook your reader.
- Describe scene.
- Introduce characters.

Middle

- Develop story with at least one specific incident or happening.
- Keep your happenings in the correct order for time.
- Include descriptions.
- Here is where your action takes place.
- A conversation might work well here.
- This is a good place for a simile or two or even a bit of humor.

End

- Bring story to a close, referring to events in the story for continuity.
- Wrap it up with a satisfying ending, a zinger, or a humorous comment to leave your reader with a feeling of completion.

Useful Devices

Transitions

Most states require the use of transitions in the essays as well as in the narrative stories. Transitions make it clearer to the reader that the writer is sticking to the topic. They establish a definite organizational pattern, and make the essay or story more coherent and flowing. The use of these connective devices, however, should not be boring or repetitive. Students should be encouraged to be creative and not stick to the traditional "first," "second," third," and "finally."

Following is a partial list of transitions. Perhaps you can introduce a few of them each day to accustom your students to their use.

Interesting Transitions

speaking _____ly (refers to previous topic)

talking about _____ (again refers to previous topic)

and so it follows that.....

moving on from _____, we come to _____

in view of the fact that.....

taking into account that.....

Other Useful Transitions

similarly	likewise	thus
as compared (contrasted) to	in addition	as a result
simultaneously	concurrently	owing to
as stated above	on one hand	thanks to
consequently	on the other hand	because of
as a final point (argument)	in conclusion	afterwards

Standard, Boring Transitions (but better than none at all)

first	second	third	next
then	another	finally	

"Grabbers" — Begin Essays or Stories with.....

a quote	a good strong-verb sentence
onomatopoeia	an exclamation or interjection
a question	something humorous

"Zingers" — Conclude Essays or Stories with.....

a quote	something to make the reader think
a humorous statement	a good strong, original simile
a question	a good wrap-up sentence

3. Clustering for Ideas and Organization

Your students now know how the officials score expository/clarification and persuasive essays and short narratives. Your students also now know what good and bad essays and narratives look like. Finally, now that your students have had some experience producing the papers in groups, they are ready to practice writing the essays and stories themselves. As good English teachers, we know that good writing is preceded by good planning. Planning is especially important for the state writing assessment since so much of the score depends on the organization of the paper.

On the other hand, clustering can be dangerous since the writing tests are timed, and a few students (mostly middle-school students) spend too much time planning and do not leave enough time to write the essay or story. I have watched eighth graders try to write a rough draft in the clustering, not leaving enough time to finish writing the final essay.

Thus, we need to teach our students the art of quick-but-well-thought-out planning that organizes their thoughts in as few words and as little time as possible. To this end, if students can organize their planning by the use of a particular form of cluster, we can help them along.

Teachers in some states have a hairy problem of teaching students to cluster for narrative stories **as well as** for essays — two entirely different animals. (Other teachers have an easier job since similar planning suffices for all three types of essays required of their students.) Narrative stories require a different type of clustering from expository/clarification, descriptive, and persuasive essays. Not only do teachers have to teach their students two different kinds of clustering, but narrative writing really requires **two** types of clustering — one for topic and one for content.

Clustering for the Narrative — Topic Clustering

For the narrative essay, students have the added problem of finding a topic that dovetails with the prompt they are given. Usually students do not like the prompt and cannot think of a story idea off-hand. They need to learn to do so quickly, using their own experiences or stories remembered from past practice essays. Train them to use the same form of clustering as they did when planning the strong-verb paragraphs. However, this time they will use the cluster to find a topic.

In order to show students how to cluster to find a story idea, teach them to take the basic theme of the prompt (like **bag** for the one about the paper bag left in the classroom, a theme used twice on the fourth-grade test in Florida). Then, if they cannot immediately come up with an idea for a story, quickly cluster around it until they do find one. Here is an example.

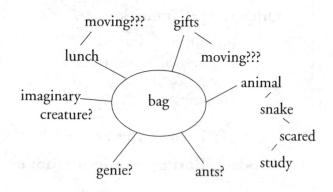

Note that the writer decided to have an animal of some sort in the bag. This was the topic he/she could pursue in the essay. **No more than 5 minutes should be spent on this cluster** since the student will need to cluster further to develop and organize his/her story. You will probably want to cluster for a topic with your class at least five times as a whole group while you direct and model the thought patterns necessary to come up with a topic in this manner. You will have to supply the prompt. (You can use the ones at the end of this section listed under the heading **210 Practice Prompts.**

Then, after you have clustered story ideas as a whole class, divide students into pairs and assign them a narrative topic. (Again, see some of the ones I put at the back of this section under the heading **210 Practice Prompts.**) Tell them to come up with a story suggestion. Students **do not** write the story at this point. They only come up with the idea for one. Next, have your pairs share their story ideas for the prompt. Repeat this procedure until you feel that your students are ready to try to cluster for story ideas on their own.

This is the point at which you bring out your timer. Working individually, students should cluster and, in five minutes or less, come up with a story idea to a prompt you supply. Practice with your students until they can do this. After each session, it is a good idea to share your students' story ideas since this will put more plots into their minds for possible future use. One of these ideas may just come in handy on the day of the test!

Now your students are ready to plan the actual story. For this, they can use the same cluster form they used to find their story idea, or they can use a type of clustering that Amy Rollo, a wonderfully innovative fourth-grade teacher at Littlewood Elementary School in Alachua

County, Florida, uses (with much success I might add) with her students. Both are described in the next section. No more than five to seven minutes should be spent on this cluster or outline.

Clustering for the Narrative — Content Clustering

Once students have a topic for the narrative essay, they need to make another plan for the organization and order of ideas for their story. This can be done in many ways, but I suggest teaching your students two ways and letting them take their choice.

The first way is to cluster in the same bubble form they used to find the topic for their story. The big bubble in the middle is the story idea. The smaller bubbles surrounding it contain the main events that will occur in the story. The roots that extend from those bubbles are the details and planned conversations that will enhance the event listed in the bubble. As in the cluster for the strong-verb paragraph, the smaller bubbles in this cluster need to be numbered to organize the order of events in the story, an element that is so important for a good score on this type of paper. Here is an example of the content cluster for the topic about finding a

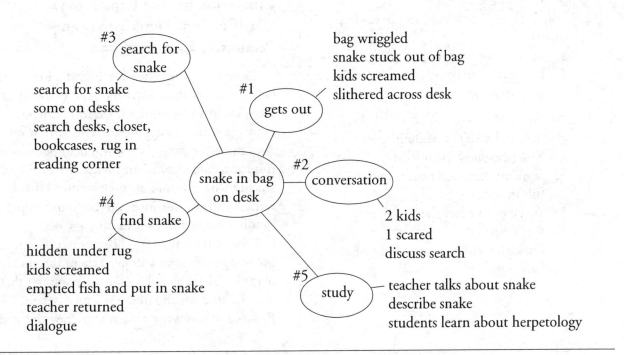

#3 search for snake

search for snake
some on desks
search desks, closet,
bookcases, rug in
reading corner

#1 gets out

bag wriggled
snake stuck out of bag
kids screamed
slithered across desk

snake in bag on desk

#2 conversation

2 kids
1 scared
discuss search

#4 find snake

hidden under rug
kids screamed
emptied fish and put in snake
teacher returned
dialogue

#5 study

teacher talks about snake
describe snake
students learn about herpetology

paper bag with something wriggling in it on the teacher's desk.

The second type of clustering used by Amy Rollo's students is that of a semi-outline that was adapted from an idea in *Write for Power*, by J. E. Sparks. She teaches her students to plan out their narratives using numbers. Students use the number one to indicate a main idea, a number two to add some detail, and a number three to get down to the nitty-gritty. Judging from the quality of the narrative papers her students produce, I would say that this is an extremely effective way of planning a narrative story. An example, using the same "bag" story follows.

1. Snake gets out of bag
   2. Bag wriggled
   2. Kids screamed
      3. Snake slithered across desk

1. Conversation held
   2. One scared and saying, "Get it out of here."
   2. One calming the other.
      3. Two kids discuss search. "Where are you going to look?"

1. Search for snake
   2. Search desks
      3. Some kids on top of desks. Others searching under
   2. Search closet, bookcases, rug in reading corner
      3. Look under and over
      3. Describe search and picture of kids all over room

1. Find snake
   2. Hidden under rug in reading corner
      3. Kids screamed when found
      3. Someone emptied fish jar and put fish in sink
      3. Snake put in fish jar
   2. Teacher returns
      3. Dialogue with teacher asking what happened

1. Teacher starts to study snakes
   2. Bag was to get students interested
   2. Teacher talks about snakes
      3. Shed skin, eating habits, kinds
      3. Students learn about herpetology

As you can see, this type of story planning is much more detailed than the basic cluster. It allows the student to almost write a rough draft of the story. The disadvantage of this type of plan is that it does not leave room for random thoughts to be inserted. Changing the order of events could get messy. The bottom line, however, is results, and Amy's regular fourth graders produce some fine examples of narrative writing using this method of planning.

If your students are being tested for the narrative form, it is wise to teach both forms of planning and let them choose which works best. Assign topics and have your students practice planning them. You can use the ones from previous years' tests or some of the ones I put at the back of this section under the heading **210 Practice Prompts.** Keep in mind that at this point students are **not** writing the story, just planning it. As before, it is always good to model the planning as a whole class, then have students plan a topic in groups and then in pairs, and finally have them plan individually.

Clustering for the Expository/ Clarification, Descriptive, and Persuasive Essays

Some innovative teacher found a form that helps organize the clustering of an essay in such a way that in a few minutes, students can have the essay planned and organized. The form itself does the organizing! I do not remember where this form came from, but my hat goes off to the teacher who invented it; my profound thanks as well! A copy of this form can be found under the heading **Essay Plan Form** on **page 42.**

You will want to run off many copies of this planning form. You will need them for practicing planning alone as well as for the planning that precedes the writing of the practice papers. Eventually you want students to draw this plan on their own since on the day of the actual test, they will have only a blank sheet of paper on which to plan.

First, introduce a topic (prompt) and teach students to plan out their essays or narratives. Your resource teacher or your county coordinator for English may have given you a number of practice prompts to use. If not, use the ones from previous years' tests or some of the ones I put at the back of this section under the heading **210 Practice Prompts**.

Another source of prompts is a brainstorming session with your fellow teachers. Just come up with some general topics to which students can relate. High school teachers can ask their students to brainstorm with them to come up with a good list.

Put the topic (prompt) on the board and pass out a copy of the **Essay Plan Form**, one per student. This planning sheet works with all grade levels. Have students place the sheet so that the single box is at the top. Into that top box goes the main essay topic. Into the three boxes in the middle go the three ideas that will be developed to support or to give details to the main topic. In the four spaces in each of the bottom boxes, students should write specific, related, supporting details or examples (depending on the type of essay) to develop the more general idea in the middle box above it.

You may want to start by doing this together at least four times with four different prompts (two of each kind of essay that will be tested) before turning your students loose to use this form of clustering on their own. Tell them to use words, not complete sentences. This is a plan, not a rough draft of the essay. **Please note:** at this stage, no essays are being written. Students will do that later. Now they are getting used to planning.

After practicing planning as a large group, students are ready to plan in smaller groups. Divide your class into groups of four and assign at least another two or three prompts to use for planning purposes in the small groups. After this practice, students should be ready to plan and write essays on their own.

> **NOTE:** *Elementary teachers may want to have students practice the planning several more times. It is a good idea to set a timer for five minutes in order to train them to cluster fairly quickly. You have to train them to think quickly and to limit planning of the essay or story to 10 minutes. This time limit may include two clusters (for a narrative), a quickie of the type needed to find the topic (see earlier section, Topic Clustering) and then the second cluster or semi-outline to come up with the details of the story.*

Essay Plan Form

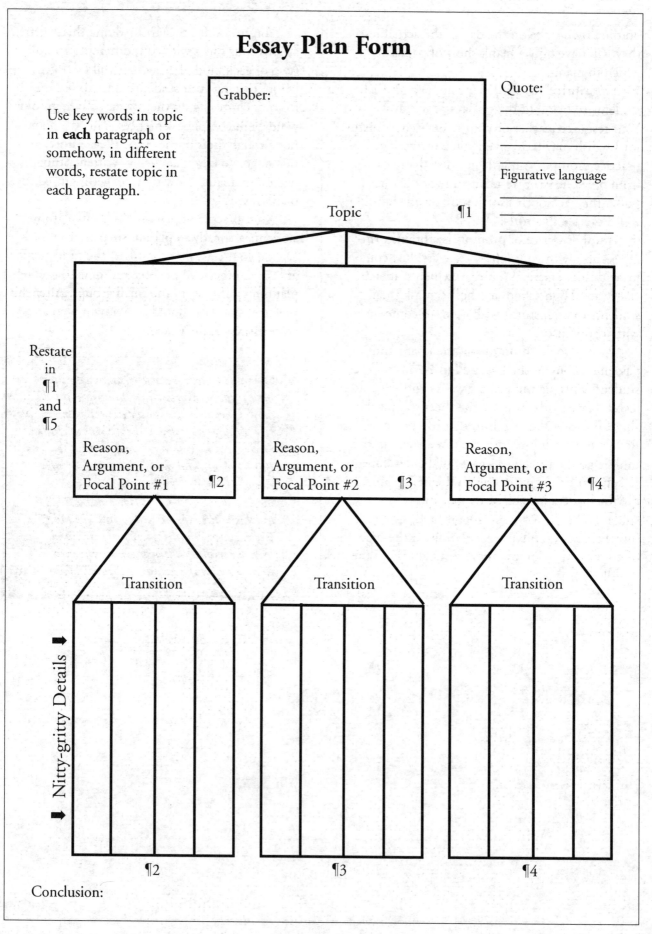

Use key words in topic in **each** paragraph or somehow, in different words, restate topic in each paragraph.

Grabber:

Topic   ¶1

Quote:

_____
_____
_____
_____

Figurative language

_____
_____
_____

Restate in ¶1 and ¶5

Reason, Argument, or Focal Point #1   ¶2

Reason, Argument, or Focal Point #2   ¶3

Reason, Argument, or Focal Point #3   ¶4

Transition

Transition

Transition

Nitty-gritty Details

¶2

¶3

¶4

Conclusion:

4. Restating the Topic (Finding the Key Words)

In most states, if a student does nothing but write one paragraph in which he or she restates the topic, he or she will earn a score of at least a **1**. Thus, it is of extreme importance to teach your students to restate the topic, at a minimum, in the first paragraph. You can practice this very easily by giving your students topic after topic and asking them to practice restating it. I ask my students to go one step farther.

There is, what I call, "the Gifted Hole" into which many bright students stumble. Their minds usually do not focus on one thing, but on many things at once. Sometimes they can write a word (any word-usually a noun), and a flood of ideas comes to mind. Unfortunately, when writing their essays, they often go off on these tangents and make the most egregious error they can possibly make on a writing test; they get off the topic!

To prevent this, it is a good idea to teach your students, "gifted" and "regular," to restate the topic in some fashion in every paragraph of the essay or story. In this way, they not only remind the reader of the focus of the paper, but, more importantly, the writers remind themselves not to stray from its path. Now, restating the topic each paragraph has its own hazards--boredom. You do not want your students to keep writing, "Another reason Spring is my favorite season is..." or "My next argument why students should wear uniforms is..." This rings the death knell of high scores in the State of Florida. If students bore the scorer by this type of dull, uninspired repetition, they will earn a boring score of a **3** for their monotonous and lackluster paper.

So, how do you restate the topic without boring the reader and writing a lifeless, bland essay or story? The answer is "key words." If students can find the one or two key words in a prompt and somehow integrate them into the middle of the text of each paragraph, they will avoid dullness. By the way, whenever, one of my students does write as the first line of each paragraph, "Another reason my eighth-grade year is my favorite year..." or the like, I draw a nose by the sentence when I score the paper.

A nose symbolizes the International Sign Language for "boring." This sign consists of twisting your right index finger gently back and forth on the right side of your nose. I teach this sign to my students at the beginning of the year and we use the symbol as needed. I sometimes see students use themselves as they write, then go back and erase the offending line.

In each prompt, one can find the one or two key words that need to be woven into the text of each paragraph. In a narrative, it is usually the last word or the word that follows "about a." In a descriptive essay, it is the thing being described. In an expository/clarification essay, it is the topic being explained plus the word "why" or "reason." In a persuasive or point of view essay, it is the word "convince" or "persuade" plus the word that is the crux of the essay.

Examples of Key Words in Prompts

In the following partial prompts (of which I have stated only the meat of the topic), the key words are highlighted.

Descriptive:
Describe the place where you go to find **peace** when you are upset.
Describe your favorite **food**.
Describe the most **beautiful scene** in nature that you can imagine.
Describe a place where you can have **fun**.
Describe your favorite **season** (or the **name of that season**).

Expository/Clarification:
Explain what are the traits that make a **good friend**.
Explain why your **favorite season** is your favorite.
Explain some **solutions** to this environmental problem.
Explain why eating **healthy foods** is important.
Explain why you think it is important to **learn to read**.

Narrative:

Imagine that you were a pioneer and tell a story about a time when you traveled on a **wagon train** that was pulled by horses.

Tell a story about what was in that **bag** on your teacher's desk.

Tell a story about what was on the other side of that **door**.

Tell a story about a **day** in which everything went wrong.

Tell a story about what would happen if you were your **favorite character** (or the character's name) in your favorite book.

Persuasive/Point of View:

Do you think the **drop-out age** should be raised to 18?

Should **homework be eliminated** on weekends?

Convince your reader to adopt your **suggestion** (or **name suggestion**).

Should **uniforms** be required in public schools?

Convince your parents to allow you to have this **pet**.

To practice finding the key words, I suggest using the "hat practice" explained in **Section 6** of this chapter. Copy the pages in this book that list the prompts you wish to use and then cut out appropriate topics. Fold them and put them in a "hat" for your students to draw upon. I suggest doing only one or two a day so this does not become hackneyed to your students. After a student draws the prompt, ask the class to ferret out the key words in that topic.

When your students cluster or write a story or essay, ask them to identify the key words. Do this until they can find them on their own. For a while, ask your students to circle the key words in their writing. This will make them aware of their use. Don't be afraid to use the nose...

5. Beginning with the Beginning (Opening Paragraphs)

Now that your students know what constitutes a good essay or story and how to cluster for one, they need to begin the actual writing process of producing a top-scoring paper. To begin this process, it is a good idea to start with the beginning - the "grabber." This is the first thing that a reader sees in a paper. This is the "hook" that makes the reader want to finish reading the piece.

I tell my students that this is a vital part of achieving a high score because without that scorer's initial interest, that student's essay or story will read like the thousands of others the scorer has read that day. It is important to "wake up" the reader, to make that scorer gasp and say right out loud in the hushed quiet of rustling papers being read, "Wow, folks, I have a live one here!!!!!"

To achieve the goal of sinking that initial "hook" into the reader requires practice. Thus it is a good idea to hand students a topic, such as the common expository one, "Explain why your favorite season is your favorite." An excellent practice is to take such an uninspiring topic and make students write an introductory paragraph for each of the four seasons, espousing that each one in turn is, indeed, the student's favorite season. Then instruct students that each introductory paragraph must begin in a different way. I list them on the board.

- Begin with a brief conversation.
- Begin with onomatopoeia.
- Begin with an appropriate quotation (made up or a real one).
- Begin with a brief narrative episode that leads into the topic

Students get to pick which season to put with which type of "grabber," but you will notice that fall almost always gets the onomatopoeia.

The rest of each introductory paragraph must restate the prompt cleverly, somehow creatively indicate the three explanations, arguments, or focal points that would be developed if the essay were being written, and conclude with a sentence that wraps it all up in a nice bow and perhaps leads to a theme that could be continued in the rest of the essay. All this must be done cleverly, not in a boring, rote fashion, "The three reasons why I like Spring the best are....."

This same practice can be done for a narrative. After the "grabber," (and you can ask students to write four different grabbers for the same narrative topic), students must launch into the beginning of their story, making sure that they restate the prompt.

I like to repeat this exercise at least four times with different topics/prompts. You can find 210 of these listed that begin on **page 51**. Students save these first paragraphs so that in the next stage of **Step Three** in which they write the *entire* essay or story, they can use some of them to begin a full essay or story. In having to look through their folders and re-read their introductory paragraphs, students get used to the idea that they must begin their writing in an interesting way.

Another idea can be found on **page 47**. This is the **Evaluation Writing** activity that includes identifying the "grabber."

6. Learning to Produce Nitty-gritty Detail in the Middle

Many activities can be used to teach students how to use nitty-gritty detail in an essay or story. Nitty-gritty detail is the bane of most writing teachers' existence. In other parlance it is called elaboration. Teachers from grades one through twelve have told me of their struggles to eke this out of many of their students. Students do not elaborate for several reasons, one being that they simply don't know how! Others range from laziness to the difficulty of getting the details and pictures that are in one's head down onto the paper in actual writing. Whatever the reason(s), the following activities may help. Elaboration is the key to higher scores. In all states that conduct a writing test, a student cannot get anything but the lowest score without elaboration. I call elaboration *nitty-gritty detail* because my students can relate better to that term.

Teaching Students What Exactly Is Nitty-gritty Detail

This is hard. While some books on writing include worksheets on the subject, I tend to shy away from them. Worksheets never taught my students much that they retained and understood on a profound level. I like to teach by practice, repetition, and example. First, I use examples from any reading selection we have on hand. You can find nitty-gritty detail in a book as simple as *Winnie the Pooh* when Pooh, for example, talks about the bees. In more sophisticated reading material or literature, finding nitty-gritty detail is even easier. I'll never forget Maya Angelou's detailed picture of life for an African-American child in the 1930s in Stamps, Arkansas, with examples galore to illustrate her point.

So, what is nitty-gritty detail? Simply stated, it is giving specific incidents or examples that support any statement that you make. Examples from previous students' papers also can be used to show nitty-gritty detail. A prime example that I found in a student's essay included as the topic sentence of one of the middle paragraphs, "I would like to be Melissa for one day because she is an only child, while I have to deal with a sister who messes in my room." This is a statement that has little meaning without some details, some examples of exactly **how** her sister messes in her room. What, in fact, does "messes in my room" mean? The student continued after her topic sentence, "My sister plays with my CDs, gets into my closet and tries on my clothes, and takes my stuffed animals from my bed." *That* is the nitty-gritty detail that supports her basic statement that her sister "messes in her room."

Other excellent student examples of elaboration can be found in the last section of this book where you can find fifty-three stories and essays that were written by students in grades four, seven, eight, and ten. Read your students the nitty-gritty detail in the high-scoring ones. **Example #7 of Sample #2 — Expository/ Clarification — "Book"** is a good one to use. In this superlative essay, the student supports almost every statement he makes. For example, he says he likes the book because "the action never stops." He then goes on to include his nitty-gritty detail. "There is trickery as Napoleon manages to change the basic rules of the new farm and treachery as he gets rid of Snowball." He could have said, "There is trickery and treachery." This would not be nitty-gritty detail. He has to get into the plot of the book with examples to illustrate his point. *That* is good elaboration, good writing.

To illustrate the point even further, take any of the "telling, dead-verb sentences" on the worksheets in **Step One** and ask your students to provide some examples and details to illustrate that topic sentence. Essentially, if you have used this book step-by-step, you have already taught your students about nitty-gritty detail when they wrote all those strong-verb paragraphs! That is exactly what strong-verb paragraphs are — elaboration (nitty-gritty detail) about a topic ("telling") sentence.

Further Analysis of Other Writing

To help with practice in locating detail and other things in any passage that I may ask my students to read, I provide them with a sheet to fill out as we read (**see next page**.) I got this idea from Marcie Freeman's book, *Listen to This*. My students enjoy analyzing poems, essays, etc., using the following form. They work first in groups and then individually. Sometimes I put the form on the overhead, and we analyze a selection as an entire class. On the following page, you will find an example of the sheet to use in evaluating essays. You can, of course, modify this evaluation device and leave out the parts you don't wish to emphasize at this point in time.

"Hat" Practice with Nitty-gritty Detail

Besides pointing out examples in the books your students read, in student examples, and in the strong-verb paragraphs, you can play games to elicit the desired details from your students. Make a copy of the prompts in **Section #10,**

210 Practice Prompts of this chapter. Cut them up. Put them in a box or a big hat and mix them up. Ask a student at random to pull a topic from the hat. After the class has determined what type of writing is required - narrative, expository, descriptive, persuasive - elicit from that child (and subsequently the class) one of the scenes, explanations, focal points, or arguments that could be used to write a paper from this topic. Then ask for detail to support or detail that scene, explanation, focal point, or argument.

For example, if the student pulls up the topic "Explain whether you prefer living in a large city or a small town," elicit first the type of writing. (It is, of course, expository.) Then go on to ask for a choice - small town or big city. Let's say your student picks "big city." Now elicit one reason why he/she chose the big city. Maybe the student would say, "Because there are many things to do in a big city." *Now* you have your topic sentence from which to work.

At this point I like to place my hand, palm up, in front of me and curl my fingers back and forth as if inviting more and more detail (or like using the symbol for the Italian word "Ciao"). This hand motion is my signal for my students to get busy providing detail about a topic sentence. For this topic, you would want your students to come up with nitty-gritty detail of exactly what things you *can* do in a big city. "Big cities have many skating rinks, lots of movie theaters for choices, and even ramps for skateboards." I don't let my students stop there. I go on and elicit at least five more examples of details that could come from that one simple sentence about "the many things to do in a big city."

This exercise will work with any of the 210 prompts you find in **Section #10, 210 Practice Prompts**. It is a good idea to do no more than one or two a day over a period of several weeks. Students will soon get the hang of it, and you will find that the elaboration carries over into their writing.

Evaluating Writing

Function: _____

Organization (paragraphs, stanzas, etc): _____

Beginning: "Grabber" _____

        Statement of Topic _____

Explanations, Focal Points, or Arguments:

        1. _____

        2. _____

        3. _____

List 4 of the Supporting Details: _____

_____

Lively Writing and Figurative Language:

    Strong Verbs Used: _____

    Great Vocabulary: _____

    Literary Devices Used: _____

    Other Lively Writing: _____

Interesting Part of Ending: _____

_____

More Practice with Nitty-gritty Details

If your students need even more practice with elaboration (nitty-gritty detail), here's another activity that brings the point home. Take your students' essays or narratives. As you read them, keep a piece of paper next to you and write down any "telling," unsupported topic sentence. You will soon have a list. After pointing out to your students that these examples are from their own papers, elicit the nitty-gritty details that were lacking in the original papers. No student need know from whose papers the examples come. The class as a whole must suggest details and examples.

You can carry this one step further. Read one of the "telling" sentences you took from your students' writing. Write it on the board. Ask your students to get out pencil and paper and, after they have completed a few sentences in groups, ask them to write, individually, at least three nitty-gritty details for that sentence.

Students Need Even More Practice??

Have them take an essay, preferably one that they wrote themselves. Then, using the **Essay Plan Form** included in **Section #5**, instruct them to try to fill out the plan sheet, especially the bottom part in which they list the nitty-gritty details. If they cannot find any details in the essay to list there, ask them to think of some appropriate examples and then rewrite the essay, putting in the elaboration they neglected to put in the first time they wrote it.

Another idea? Go back and repeat **Step One** of this book and have your students write more strong-verb paragraphs.

7. Ending with a Bang

Students tend to peter out towards the end of an essay or story. Their conclusions often leave something to be desired. I tell my students that the ending is just as important as the beginning. They must really end with a bang! They want that official scorer to stand up and say, "Look, folks, I've got a live one here." They also want to

keep me (who must read 1200 to 1500 essays between August and January) from being bored. Boring essays do not earn high scores.

Learning to practice ending with a bang or a "zinger" is more difficult than getting students to begin with a "grabber." This is where a well-placed quote works well. A good ending conversation might not be amiss either. Ending with a question is also good. In fact, anything that works well as a "grabber" works equally well as a "zinger."

For practice, I read (or give my students to read) an essay that lacks an ending. Students must then write the end, coming to a satisfying end that brings the story full circle in a narrative and restating the three reasons, focal points, or arguments in an expository, descriptive, or persuasive essay. They must then elaborate on this to come up with a final bang or "zinger" that leaves the reader laughing, wondering, or otherwise engaged. The kiss of death in my class is for a student to find a nose beside their conclusion. This is the symbol in the International Sign Language for "boring."

For this exercise, I simply print up examples from the ones in the last section of this book, only I take off the last paragraph. I also use my own students' essays, again taking off the name and the conclusion. You should repeat this practice until students can write satisfying and interesting conclusions.

Again, as in practice for the introductory paragraph, you could use the **Evaluation Writing** sheet on **page 47**.

8. Procedure for Practicing the Actual Writing

Now that students can plan an essay and a narrative, write a good introduction, use transitions, and produce nitty-gritty detail, it is time to write. Provide an **Essay Plan Form** sheet **(See page 42)** if the topic is expository/clarification or persuasive and assign a topic. (See the suggested topics at the end of this **Step** under the heading **Practice Prompts.**) Give students

45 minutes to cluster and write their essay or story. Encourage students to be enthusiastic.

You will need to provide students with one of the **Essay Plan Form** sheets (**page 42**) for the next few times they write essays. They will soon be willing, indeed prefer, to make one on their own just as they will have to do on the actual test. Encourage this practice.

Do not let students put their names on their papers. Instead, assign each student a number. It is a good idea to use the number in your gradebook that is by each student's name. This will make it easier for you to record the results. You should plan to have students write at least fifteen essays or stories before the actual day of the test. Don't flinch at this point. The grading is not hard or time-consuming. Read on....

9. Grading the Essays/Narratives

Collect each set of completed papers. **You** holistically score it on the high-medium-low or the six-point rubric given in **Step Two**. Write the score in very small script in the lower-left corner on the **back** of each student's paper. Then fold over the corner so that the students cannot inadvertently see your score as **they** attempt to score the paper for practice. Doing this will give the students confirmation that their scoring efforts were accurate (or not) and will help them learn to judge their writing efforts.

Another method that I am trying this year (that seems to be working even better) is to reduce the size of the **Focused Analytical Scoring Sheet (page 24)** to where it can fit three on a single page. At the bottom I write "High, Medium, Low." I then make many copies so that the students can attach one to the top of each essay and then I grade the essays, using that form. Comments can be made by putting checks in the appropriate places on the **Focused Analytical Scoring Sheet** (saving time) and scores can be assigned by circling one of the numbers at the bottom. I then fold over the sheet and staple it closed so that students cannot cheat when they themselves score the paper. I usually score the papers first simply because I

collect them at the end of the period and have time to score them while the next class is writing. In that way, the papers can be returned to the students the next day when it is **their** turn to score.

> **NOTE:** *Do not be afraid to score your students' essays. Scoring on a high, medium, low scale is very easy after you have read a few papers. Also, do not be intimidated by the large number of practice papers you have to grade. In my workshops, I ask the teachers to score between 30 and 40 essays in approximately the same number of minutes. While my students write the essays, I (and most of my colleagues as well) can score over 400 essays a week and not take a single paper home! Scoring holistically is a lot different from regular paper grading. You are only skimming each paper, not reading it thoroughly. It should take less than a minute per paper to read. You are looking for an impression, not a detailed analysis. If it takes you longer than one minute per essay, your skimming skills might be rusty. Remember, the actual scorers on your state's writing test take no more than that themselves!*

After **you** score the papers, the next day in class review the criteria for scoring in each of the four elements that should be included in a good essay or narrative. Hand out the papers, telling students that if they get their own, they should hand it to someone else. If you have several classes, it is a good idea to have students score the papers of a different class. Each student should have an example to score.

Hand out a copy of the **Focused Analytical Score Sheet** (found on **page 24**) to each student. Divide the class into groups of four and have the groups collectively score the papers that each student in that group holds. Walk around the room to arbitrate disputes or resolve problems. Elementary teachers may be able to suspend reading groups for a few weeks in order to do this. After all, students **are** reading. This would increase time spent practicing for the test.

After each scoring session, hold a discussion. Ask students to unfold the corner of the back of the paper or expose the stapled scoring sheet to see the score **you** gave the paper. (Remember, on a 6-point scale, **High** is equivalent to **5** or **6**, Medium is equivalent to **3** or **4**, **Low** is equivalent to **1** or **2**, and **Zero** is the same as **unscorable** On a 5-point scale, **high** is eqivilent to a **4.5** or **5**, **medium** is the same as a **3** or **4**, and a **low** equals a **1** or **2**. The 4-point scale is self-evident.) Discuss any glaring differences between your scores and those of your students by scoring the paper once more by a consensus of the class. After grading about five papers in this manner, students are ready to analyze and score a few of their own efforts.

This year, instead of having students score anonymous papers, I am using the writing response groups (four students heterogeneously grouped by competency in English) to score their own papers. Each student in a group reads his or her own essay to his/her peers, and the group debates and then decides the score. This seems to be very effective, as students are learning more quickly from participating in scoring their own essays. Keep in mind, however, that this year I have a particularly amiable group of students who work well together and who, for the most part, take each others' writing efforts seriously. I do not recommend using this method if your students will make fun of each other's writing. We still hold the whole class discussion of the results after all the papers are scored and after the students see the scores I assigned to their papers.

More Practice

The final part of **Step Three** is to conduct a blitz of essay writing. (Fourth-grade teachers in some states would have to do two shorter blitzes, one of expository/clarification essays and one of narratives.) I usually do this a month before the actual test. My eighth-grade students spend three to four weeks doing the following:

Monday

Plan and write an essay or narrative in class. Spend no more than 45 minutes. Teacher finishes scoring previous day's essays.

Tuesday

Students get into groups and score essays, putting "high, medium, low, or zero" in the upper left-hand corner of the paper. Any questions can be referred to the teacher. Students can be asked to score them blind or to score their own papers in a consensus with their response group. High-school teachers may want to have students score on the six-point rubric. Discuss results.

Wednesday

Same as Monday.

Thursday

Same as Tuesday.

Friday

Same as Monday.

After you have scored at least five essays or narratives for each student, you probably will be ready to scream, and your eyes will be crossing. So that you don't have to continue to score **every** paper your students write, or when you reach the point that you can't stand to score another paper without suffering from extreme nausea at the very thought of it, try the following.

When students have completed and scored two or three essays or narratives, have them pick the **one** they think is the best and hand it to you to score. In this way, you have to grade only **one in two or three**. This makes the scoring more manageable. Also, in requiring students to score their own papers **before** handing them in to you, you are asking your students to take the final step and actually analyze their own papers without any crutches at all. Now they are ready for **Step Four**.

10. 210 Practice Prompts

Introduction

The following suggested prompts come from a variety of sources. Some are actual test topics from various states. Others were written by other teachers or by the former Alachua County Supervisor of English, Mary Anne Coxe. Still others came to me by word of mouth, via students, of practice test prompts they encountered over the years. I wrote most of the remainder to use with my students.

Whatever the source, these practice prompts are included here to be used to cluster, to write, to practice topic recognition or produce nitty-gritty detail (cut up and put into a hat), or to discuss as possible topics that could appear on the real state writing assessment test.

Since these prompts work for all grades, you will wish to make the actual wording of the prompts more specific for the third/fourth and seventh/eighth grades, and more general and open-ended for the tenth grade. You also may wish to simplify a prompt or make it more sophisticated, depending on your students. Some may not be appropriate for your grade level. Pick and choose among them for practice topics.

Some of the prompts offer alternative versions for younger students since many states recycle topics from elementary to middle to high school, changing the wording a bit.

Since different states present the prompts in different formats, I have reduced many of the topics to their basic content, the part that tells the students about what they are to write. When you use one of these prompts, **expand it** to fit the usual format **your** state writing assessment test uses, or your students may be confused when they see the long introduction and instructions on the actual test. Some states even include a story or essay that sets the scene for the topic! Remind students that usually the **last sentence of the prompt** actually tells them what to write. Some of the following suggested prompts are equivalent to those last sentences on the actual test. Others are more wordy and try to mimic actual test questions.

Please note that although the following prompts are, by necessity, generic, you will find that the potential pitfalls that usually occur with actual test prompts are amply represented. The most obvious and potentially dangerous (score-wise) of these pitfalls is the one in which a prompt asks for one part to be explained but mentions other parts. For example, "There are many environmental problems that plague our world. Pick one of these problems and propose some solutions to it." Or, "If you could pick one item of your school's dress code to change, what would it be? Write an essay to convince your school's administration to change that item." Many students see the words "environmental problems" or "dress code" and get off the topic by writing about a bunch of problems or argue about the dress code in general.

You will notice that I have included more expository/clarification and persuasive prompts than narrative or descriptive ones. Since most states require that students at **all** the grade levels that are tested compose an expository/clarification essay, I have included many more examples of this type to give you a wider choice. Also, since the persuasive essay is often the hardest to write and usually the type on which students score the lowest, more prompts of this type are included.

Good luck on the actual test!

40. Descriptive Prompts for Elementary, Middle, and High Schools

NOTE: *Most states do not ask students to describe people, so only one prompt of this type is included in the suggested topics. Some states require that students write only a visual description and others ask students to include other senses such as feel, touch, smell, and taste. You will need to modify these prompts to fit the requirements of your particular state.*

1. Describe a place you always wanted to visit.

2. Describe the most beautiful scene in nature that you can imagine.

3. Describe a kitchen that you have seen or would like to see.

4. Describe the ocean. Think about what it looks like on and below the surface.

5. Describe a storm. This could be a thunder storm, a snowstorm, a hurricane, a tornado, a hail storm, a rain storm, or any type of storm.

6. Describe a place where you feel safe and protected.

7. Describe a toy you love(d). Think of all its good points.

8. Describe your ideal playground.

9. Describe the perfect shopping mall.

10. Describe a place where people congregate (like a zoo, a church, a circus, etc.)

11. Describe your bedroom the way you want it to be.

12. Describe your favorite dessert (or food).

13. Describe a beach (a desert, a mountain, a city, or a plain).

14. Think of your favorite animal and describe that animal.

15. Describe your best friend so that the reader can picture him or her.

NOTE: *An attempt has been made to phrase the last twenty-five prompts as they might appear on the test. Use them as you see fit. In many states, on the actual test, these prompts would be divided into three separate paragraphs. In the interest of space, I have omitted these separations and have written each prompt as one paragraph. Write them for your students the way they might appear on your state's writing test.*

16. Think of your favorite place. What do you like about this place? What do you do there? How does it look, smell, and feel? Now write an essay describing your favorite place so that your reader will be able to picture it.

17. Some people prefer dogs as pets, some like cats, and others prefer birds, snakes, fish, rabbits, pigs, horses, and other animals. What is your perfect pet? What does it look like? Is it soft or hard? Does it make any sounds? Now describe your idea of a perfect pet so that your reader can picture it.

18. Different teachers decorate their classes in different manners. Think of your idea of the perfect classrooms. Is it colorful? Does it have desks or tables? What does it look like? How does it smell? Are there any sounds in it? Write an essay describing your idea of the perfect classroom.

19. Each season of the year is beautiful in some way. Think of which season is your favorite: winter, summer, spring, or fall. Think of what your town looks like during that season. Think of the sounds you hear outside during that season. What does it feel like? Is there a smell or a taste to it? Now write an essay describing an outdoor scene during your favorite season of the year.

20. Everyone has a favorite object that they treasure. Think of some object in your room that you really like. It could be a toy, or a doll, a game, a stuffed animal, or a book, but whatever it is, it is special to you. What does it look, feel, smell, and sound like? Now, describe this object to your reader so that he or she will be able to picture it clearly.

21. Every person has a favorite place to play. Think of your favorite place to play. It may be your backyard, or a playground, or a nearby woods, or an open field. What does this place look like? What are the sounds you hear there? What does it feel and smell like? Describe your favorite place to play so that your reader can see it without being there.

22. Almost all houses have kitchens. Some are big and some are tiny. Think of the kitchen at your home. Think of how you might change it to make it even better. What is in it? What does it smell like? Now, describe this perfect kitchen to your reader so that he or she can see it clearly.

23. There are trees everywhere, even in the middle of big cities. Think of a tree you have seen. What does it look, feel, and sound like? Describe that tree so that your reader can picture it, too.

24. People gather at places like malls, fairgrounds, schools, gymnasiums, sports fields, and swimming pools. Think of a place in your town where there are lots of people. How does it look, sound, smell, and feel to be there? Now, describe that crowded place so that your reader can feel as if he or she is there.

25. Every child enjoys playing on a playground. Think of the playgrounds you have played in. Think of what makes them better. Maybe you've already seen it, but think of what makes the perfect playground. Think of how it looks, sounds, feels, and smells. Now, describe your idea of a perfect playground so that your reader can see it clearly.

26. Even in the desert it rains sometimes. Think of what the world looks like outside your window when it rains. Think about how it looks, smells, and feels. What sounds do you hear? What does rain taste like? Describe what the world looks like outside a window when it rains.

27. Flowers always make a yard or a room look very pretty. Think of a garden or a bunch of flowers you have seen. Make it even better and prettier in your mind. What does it look and feel like? Does it smell? Describe that garden or bunch of flowers so that your reader can see it and smell it in his or her mind.

28. Cities and towns have lots of things going on in them, lots of stores, traffic, people, churches, schools, parks, and maybe even a zoo. Think of your city or a city you have visited. As you walk down the sidewalk in the middle of that city what do you see, hear, smell, taste, and feel? Describe that city for your reader and what it is like to be there.

29. Even in big cities, there are parks where there are woods. There are woods everywhere in this big country of ours. Think of a woods you have been in or played in. What does it look like? Now describe this woods so that the reader can see it.

30. Alice visits Wonderland in Alice in Wonderland. Wonderland is the land of her dreams. What is the ideal place for you. What place do you dream about? What does it look like? Does it have a smell? How does it feel? Do you hear sounds there? Describe the ideal place of your dreams in such a way that the reader can picture it, too.

31. We all eat to stay alive, but everyone has a favorite food. What is your favorite food in the world? What does it look like? How does it smell and taste in your mouth? Describe your favorite food so that your reader can see it and almost taste it as well.

32. Many people love the beach and others love the mountains for a vacation. Which do you like better, the beach or the mountains?. Even if you have never been to either, you have seen pictures. Choose one — either a beach or the mountains. What does this place look like? Does the place have a feel to it? What smells are there? What sounds do you hear? Describe your beach or mountains so that your reader can picture the scene you see in your mind.

33. Everyone has a favorite game, dominoes, checkers, cards, Clue, Chutes and Ladders, Monopoly, and so on. What is your favorite game? What does it look like when you play? What sounds do you hear as you play? Describe your favorite game so that the reader can see it and hear the action as you play.

34. Everyone has to shop for food or clothes sometime. Think of a store to which you like to go. What does it look like inside the store? Are there sounds? What do things feel like there? Does the store have a smell? Write a description of a store you like to visit so that your reader can feel as if he or she were there.

35. People live in houses, apartments, tents, cabins, trailers, and other buildings. Where do you live? Think of your ideal living place. Perhaps it's where you live now. What does it look like? Does it have a smell? Describe your ideal living place or the place where you live so that your reader can picture it clearly.

36. Imagine that you were on a ship in the middle of the ocean. What does your ship look like? How does the ocean look? What does the sky look like above you? What do you see, hear, feel, smell, and taste as you look about. Describe your ship in the middle of an ocean of water.

37. Everyone has been in a thunder storm. Think back to when you last experienced a thunder storm. What was it like? What were the sights, sounds, smells, and tastes, and feelings during the storm. Describe a thunder storm so that your reader can experience and picture it.

38. Imagine that someone gave you a very special ring. What does this ring look like as it sits on your finger? How does it feel? Is it heavy? Is there a taste to it? How does it sound if you rap it on the desk? Does it smell? Describe this special ring down to the last detail so that your reader can picture it on your hand.

39. Our country has a flag with fifty stars representing the fifty states and thirteen stripes representing the thirteen colonies. Your State has a flag, too, with things on it that represent important historical events and items of your state. Imagine that you had a flag which represented you. What would it look like? How does it feel? Does it have a smell? Does it make a sound as it waves in a breeze? Think of some images it would have on it to represent you to the world. Now, describe your personal flag so that your reader can see it clearly.

40. Almost everyone has had an encounter with a spider, has read the book, *Charlotte's Web*, and has seen pictures of spiders in their webs. Think of a spider and web you have seen. It could have been real, in a book, or in your imagination. What do this spider and web look like? Do they make a sound? What do they feel like if you touch them?
Do they have a smell? Now, describe your spider and its
web so vividly that your reader can see it as if it were
right in front of him or her.

65 Expository/Clarification Prompts for Elementary, Middle, and High Schools

NOTE #1: *Stress in expository/clarification topics that the main part of the essay should be devoted to the <u>last</u> thing asked. Usually this is to propose solutions or to explain why. Descriptions and explanations of choice of items should be written in the introduction. You must make this clear to your students, or you could have a few of them ignore the main thrust of the topic.*

NOTE #2: *Since all grades that are tested require that students write an expository/clarification essay, I have included many more prompts for practice.*

1. Write about what you think the world will be like in 100 years.

2. We are learning all the time. Write about something you have learned recently and how it has affected you.

3. You have been asked by your principal to recommend one course which will help you prepare for the job you want in the future. It could be a course your school is already offering or a new course. Write an essay to explain to your principal the course you would recommend. Be sure to give clear reasons for your suggestion.

4. Explain the main reasons why you think students drop out of school.

5. Talk about your favorite music and why you like it.

6. Think of your favorite year in school. Explain why it was your favorite year.

7. Friends are important, but everyone has a different opinion of what makes a good friend. Explain what, in your opinion, makes a good friend.

8. Some teachers are special. Without giving any names, explain why one particular teacher in your life was so special.

9. If you could change one thing about your school, what would you change? Explain why.

10. We all get angry at times, but different people react in different ways. Some people show their anger openly, and some hide it within themselves. Explain and describe what you do when you get mad.

11. Friends sometimes experience conflicts. Explain why this happens.

12. If someone were new to your town, explain to him/her the highlights.

13. If you could make changes to your school lunchroom, what would you do?

14. Most people like one particular animal more than others. Explain why your favorite animal is your favorite animal.

15. Most people remember one day that really was special. Think about a special day you have had and write an essay explaining why that day was so special.

16. Your generation faces many problems. Identify one of these problems that you feel is the most important, explain it, and propose some possible solutions to the problem.

17. Much has been written about the negative effects of television on young people. Are all television shows bad for children? Write an essay describing a show you feel has a positive impact on today's teens and explain how this show could be helpful.

18. Rules are important in our daily lives. We have rules for driving, rules for studying, and even rules for playing. Think about the rules you have in your school. What three rules should every school have? Write an essay explaining to the reader the three rules you selected. Give clear reasons why each one is needed.

19. Games are fun and often teach us something as well. Think about your favorite game. Write a paper telling about your favorite game. Explain to the reader your reasons for enjoying it.

20. Suppose you have been appointed to a neighborhood improvement committee. You must make recommendations on ways to make your neighborhood a better place to live. Think about some changes you would like to make in your neighborhood. Write an essay to inform your reader of changes your would recommend to improve your neighborhood and why these changes are important.

21. If you could choose any animal for a class pet, what would you choose and why?

22. What is your favorite time of the year? Explain why this is your favorite time.

23. Everyone has something or someone that is important to him/her. Pick an object, a person, or a feeling that is important to you and explain why it is so important in your life.

24. Eating healthy foods is very important. Write an essay explaining why it is important to eat healthy foods.

25. Explain why it is important to learn to read.

26. Think back to when you were little and had a favorite toy. Explain why you liked this particular toy.

27. Everyone has chores to do. Explain why you do the job or chore you have.

28. If you could be any other person for a day, who would you be? Explain why you would like to be that person for a day.

29. We are increasingly worried about our environment. Write an essay explaining about one environmental problem you think is important and propose some possible solutions to the problem.

30. Suggest one change that you think can make this country better.

31. If you had a time machine and could go to any time in the past or future, where would you go? Explain why you chose that particular time.

32. Everyone has responsibilities. Write a paper explaining a responsibility you have now or will have in the future and why you shoulder that responsibility.

33. Write an essay explaining whether you prefer a big city or a small town in which to live and why you prefer it.

34. Your class is making a box to be seen in 2096. Write an essay explaining the one thing you put in that box and why.

35. Think of your favorite year in school. Now write an essay explaining why it was your favorite year.

> **NOTE:** *An attempt has been made to phrase the last thirty prompts as they might appear on the test. Use them as you see fit. In many states, on the actual test, these prompts would be divided into three separate paragraphs. In the interest of space, I have omitted these separations and have written each prompt as one paragraph. Write them for your students the way they might appear on your state's writing test.*

36. Most adults in this world have a job of some sort. Think of the ideal job for you when you complete your schooling. Now, think of some reasons why this would be your ideal job. Write an essay to explain why this is your ideal job.

37. Schools do not offer all the elective courses (like art and music) that students would like to take. Think of one elective course you want to take that your school does not offer at this time. Think of some reasons why you think this course should be offered. Now, write an essay explaining why you think that this particular elective should be offered in your high school.

38. Everyone has a book that he or she enjoyed reading, whether it be a book recently read or one read as a small child. Think of one book you have read that you really enjoyed. Maybe it was your favorite book when you were little. Maybe it's one you read recently. Think of some reasons why you liked that book. Now, write an essay explaining why you really like your favorite book.

39. Many writers, scientists, and politicians have a view of what the world will be like 50 years from now. What do you think the world will be like by the time you are in your 60's? Think of the future and the direction you think the world is headed. Write an essay explaining what you believe the world will be like 50 years from now.

40. Many students drop out of school before they graduate from high school. Think of some reasons why you think these students do not finish high school. Now, write an essay explaining why you think students drop out of school.

<u>Alternative for younger students:</u>

Many students do not do their work in school and then later often quit school before they graduate. Think of some reasons why you think these students do not do their work and get bad grades. Now, write an essay explaining why you think these students do not work in school and often quit school before graduating.

41. High school English classes require students to read Shakespeare and other classics. Some students object to this practice. Think of some reasons why you think the state requires that Shakespeare and the classics be taught in high school English. Now, write an essay explaining why you think Shakespeare and the classics are required.

<u>Alternative for younger students:</u>

In school, students must read classic books that the teacher picks. Some students do not like to be told what to read. They would rather pick their own books. Think of some reasons why your teachers require these classic books that are so famous. Think of some that your teacher has read to you or that you had to read yourself. Now, write an essay explaining why you think the teachers insist that students read and listen to the famous classics.

42. Imagine that time travel to the past was possible. Think of where and when you would like to go for a visit. Write an essay telling where and when you would go in the past and explain why you choose to go there.

43. Imagine that you had no TV or radio for one week. Think of some activities that you can do instead to keep you busy and out of trouble. Write an essay to explain what you can do to keep occupied in a week of no TV or radio.

<u>Or, alternatively if your students are having trouble with this type of essay:</u>

Imagine that you had no TV or radio for one week. Think of one activity that you would like to do instead to keep you busy and out of trouble. Write an essay explaining why you chose that one activity to replace the TV and radio for that week.

44. Teenagers (children) are faced with many problems today. School, home, society, peers all complicate your lives. Think of one problem that really bothers you. Now, think of some solutions to that problem that might make it easier to bear. Write an essay offering solutions to your worst problem.

45. Many teenagers (children) complain that adults expect too much of them. Many adults think that teenagers (children) do not help out enough at home, at school, or in society doing volunteer work. What do you think? Do adults expect too much of you? Think of some reasons to support your answer. Now, write an essay explaining whether or not you think adults expect too much of you.

46. Each year many teenagers are killed by driving under the influence of alcohol or by being a passenger in a car driven by another teen who has had too much alcohol. How can the number of alcohol-related deaths be reduced? Think of some solutions you and your friends could implement to solve this problem. What do you think would work to reduce the deaths? Now, write an essay proposing some solutions to help stop teenagers from risking their lives and driving under the influence of alcohol.

Alternative for younger students:

Each year many teenagers are killed by driving under the influence of alcohol or by being a passenger in a car driven by another teen who has had too much alcohol. Think of what you and your friends, as younger persons who cannot yet drive, can do to keep your older brothers and sisters and friends from drinking and driving when drunk. Write an essay explaining your ideas to keep these teens out of the car if they drink.

47. Pollution, excessive garbage, toxic and industrial waste, using up non-replaceable resources are all problems facing our environment. Think of one particular environmental problem that you believe could be solved. Now think of some possible solutions to that problem. Write an essay proposing and explaining your solutions to the environmental problem you chose.

48. We all have a place where we can imagine or go where we relax, let our troubles disappear, and have a good time. For some it is a place far away, and for others it is a place close to home. Think of your favorite place where you can feel an escape from the hassles of your world, a place you love to be, your favorite place. Now, write an essay explaining why this place is your favorite.

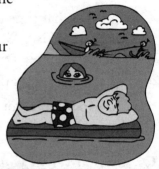

49. Everyone has something they do to relax and have fun. Some like to read; others prefer sports; still others like to chat with friends. What is your favorite thing to do to relax and have fun? Think of why you enjoy this activity so much. Now, write an essay explaining why your favorite activity is your preferred way to relax and have fun.

50. In the past few years, there have been more and more incidents of violence reported on school campuses. In fact, there have been many reports of violence even at the kindergarten level! What do you think is the cause of this rise in violence? Think of some possible reasons. Write an essay explaining why you think there have been more incidents of violence in schools in recent years.

51. By the time we reach high school, at least one teacher has made an impact on our lives. Think of a teacher you have had who influenced you and really helped you to learn and to mature. Think of some reasons why this teacher made such a positive impact on your life. Now, without mentioning the teacher's name (use Mr. or Ms. X), explain why this teacher had such a positive influence on your life.

52. Many kids hear their parents and grandparents talk about "the good old days." Is this just a figment (imaginary thought) in older people's minds as they remember their youth? Was life really better twenty or forty years ago? What do you think of this statement? Is life for teens harder now or when your parents and grandparents were young? Now, write an essay explaining your answer to this question.

53. Philosophers have written books and books about the meaning of life. Each one is different. What is your philosophy of life? What is life all about? Decide what you think are the most important elements that make us human, that are the ideas (philosophies) of the way you run your life. Write an essay explaining your philosophy of life.

Alternative for younger students:

There are many books that talk about the meaning of life. Your teacher talks about living a "good" life. What do you think are the most important things to remember to follow in the years to come? What do you think are the most important things to do in your life that will lead to your happiness? Now, write an essay explaining what will make life good and meaningful for you.

54. We all have different personalities, different ways of dealing with life, different points of view. What are the main elements of your personality. What kind of a person are you? What are you *really* like inside? Write an essay explaining your personality to your reader.

55. Life is filled with conflicts, conflicts of interest, conflicts of opinion, conflicts of life styles, etc. Most good novels have some sort of conflict in them to add to the interest. Resolving that conflict is what the novel is about. Think about some of the conflicts in your life. Now think how you resolve those conflicts. Write an essay to explain how you usually resolve conflicts. What is your method?

56. Everyone, no matter how young, has a year in his or her life that was not so good. Think of the worst year of your life. Think of reasons why it was your worst year. Write an essay explaining why that particular year was the worst year of your life.

Or conversely

Some years are better than others. Usually people can think of one that was particularly nice. Think of the best year you have had so far in your life. Think of the reasons that made it your best year. Write an essay explaining why that year was your best year yet.

57. Your school (the United States, your state, etc.) is not perfect. No matter how good something is, there are always ways to make it better. Think of one problem your school (the United States, your state, etc.) has that might be improved with some clever plans. Now, think of some solutions, some ways to make that improvement. Write an essay explaining your solutions to the problem.

58. Imagine that going to the future was possible. Think how far ahead into the future you would like to visit. Think about your reasons why you would choose that particular time. Write an essay telling how far into the future you would like to go and explain why you chose that particular time.

59. When we are young, we play games — board games, imaginary games, sports games. Think of one game you played when you were younger that you really liked. Think of some reasons why you really liked this game. Now, write an essay explaining why this game was your favorite as a younger child.

60. Medical studies have shown that exercise is a necessary part of our daily routine. What do you think? Do you exercise? Think about some reasons why you exercise. Exercising is important. Write an essay why it is important to exercise regularly.

61. We consider certain people (real or made up) to be our heros. Think about a real or made-up person and why he or she is your hero. Now write an essay explaining why that person is your hero.

62. Imagine if you could do anything you wanted for an entire week. Pick one thing you would like to do that week of freedom. Now write an essay to explain why you chose to do that one thing in a week in which you could have done anything you wished.

63. You have been told for years by your parents and teachers to eat healthy foods instead of junk food. Think of some reasons why eating healthy foods is important. Now write an essay explaining why eating healthy foods is important.

64. At school, at work, and at play we have to work in teams in order to achieve our goals. Think of some attributes that make a good team player whether it be in a sport, at work, or at school when working in groups. Now write an essay to explain what makes a person a good team player.

65. Your parents and teachers insist that respect for others is very important. Think of some reasons why this might be important. Now write an essay explaining why respect for other people is important.

45 Narrative Prompts for Elementary, Middle, and High Schools

1. Suppose you had invented a time machine. Write a story about what you did with it.

2. Write to tell of a day when you were the teacher. What did you do?

3. Write a story about trading places with your favorite TV, movie, or rock star.

4. One day a spaceship lands on the playground of your school....

5. Your shoe must have a story to tell. Tell it.

6. Your class grew plants as a science project. One day you looked at your plant and saw something really strange had grown there.

7. Write a story about what it would be like if you woke up one morning with wings.

8. On your birthday, a strange-looking lady came to your door and handed you a wrapped present. You rattled it. It made a noise. Write a story about this present.

9. Your teacher one day announced that your class was going on a wonderful field trip. Write a story about this field trip. In your story, you can have your class go anywhere you wish.

10. One day, as you were petting and talking to your friend's dog, it answered back! Write a story about this.

11. Write a story about yourself as a hero. What did you do to become a hero? Tell your story.

12. As you walked down the hallway at school, you heard some strange music coming from the custodian's closet. What was it? Write a story about it.

13. Tell a story about children who live in a world where there is no such thing as television, computers, or electronic games.

14. A distant relative bequeathed you a strange ring. As you put this ring on, you discover that it has strange powers. What does it look like? What does it do? Tell a story about this ring.

15. Tell a story about your ideal place to live. What would it be like to live there?

16. (Used twice!) The teacher comes into the room and places a bag on her desk and then leaves. The bag moves and wriggles. Write a story about what is in the paper bag.

17. Everyone has a day in his or her life that was extra special or dreams about what he or she would do on a special day. Write a story about a special day you have had or imagine you might have.

18. Every day you pass a door. It's always closed and locked. One day, as you pass, you notice that the door is open. You step inside. Write a story about what was on the other side of that door.

19. Tell a story about what happened when you traveled on a wagon pulled by horses.

20. Tell a story about a day in which everything went wrong.

> **NOTE:** *An attempt has been made to phrase the last twenty-five prompts as they might appear on the test. In many states, on the actual test, these prompts would be divided into three separate paragraphs. In the interest of space, I have omitted these separations and have written each prompt as one paragraph. Write them for your students the way they might appear on your state's writing test.*

21. Imagine you could travel to the future and live there. Think of what you think the future would be like. How different would it be from today? Now, write a story about living in the future.

22. Imagine you could go any place you wanted for as long as you wanted any time you wanted. What place would you visit? Think about what you would do there. Write a story about a visit to a really neat place.

23. Pretend that you lived in colonial times. Think about what your life would be like, how it would be different living more than 200 years ago. Now, write a story about a young person (or yourself) living in George Washington's day.

24. Novels are fun to read because the action keeps you interested, and the characters almost become your friends. Think of a book you really liked. Imagine that you were a new character in this book. Write a story about what happened.

> **NOTE:** *High school teachers might want to use a specific Shakespearean play or a specific piece of literature.*

25. Imagine you woke up one morning and found that you had switched places with a dog or a cat. Think what it would be like. What would you do? Write a story of your day as a dog or a cat.

26. What if you had a personal genie who would grant your every wish. What would your life be like? Think of some of the details. Write a story about having a personal genie.

27. Imagine you had a car that would take you anywhere you wanted to go for one day. Think of where you went in that car and what you did. Write a story about that day.

28. Everyone has a favorite season of the year. What is your favorite season? What do you like to do? Write a story about your favorite season.

29. Imagine one morning there's a knock at your front door. You open the door, and to your great surprise, you find an alien standing there. What do you do? What does it look like? Write a story about your encounter with this alien.

30. On your way to school one morning you see a huge truck speeding down the road. Suddenly, the back door of the truck opens and a large, mysterious box falls off the back of the truck. It sits there in the road. What is in the box? What do you do? Write a story about this mysterious box.

31. One spring day a skunk wanders into your classroom. What are the results? Write a story about the skunk that visited school.

32. Imagine you had a time machine that would take you only to the past. Where would you choose to go? Think of what you would do there, what it would be like. Write a story of your adventure in the past.

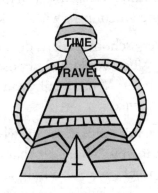

33. One day you are sitting under a large tree. An acorn hits you on the head, and you look up. There, on the branch above you sits a squirrel, laughing at you. The squirrel then looks you square in the eye, begins to talk to you, and asks you to return its acorn. What would you do? What would happen if you encountered a talking squirrel? Write a story about the experience.

34. Imagine a world where there was no money. What would people do? What would life be like? Write a story about living in a world without any money.

35. There are times when we all wish, even if just for a moment, that we could be someone else for a day. Who would you choose to be for that day? What would you do? Think of some details of your day. Now write a story about what your day was like as that person.

36. In a recent fire disaster, there were some kids who did some heroic things. Think what constitutes (makes) a hero. Imagine yourself as one. Now write a story in which you were a hero/heroine in a tough situation.

37. A little old lady gave you and a friend some magical glitter and told you to sprinkle it on your hair and something special would happen. What happened when you tried it? Write a story about this mysterious magical glitter.

38. One day you and your friends walked up to an old, seemingly abandoned house. You couldn't see inside due to the dust and cobwebs on the windows. You decide to see if the door is locked. You try the knob, and it turns. The door creaks open as if it has not opened in years..... What happens next? What do you find? What do you and your friend do? Write a story about entering that old, seemingly abandoned house.

39. Love comes in all forms. We can love our parents, a boy friend or girlfriend, a favorite pet, a brother or sister, a place, even a thing. Think about someone or something you love. Write a story about that person or thing that involves your feelings.

40. Imagine that your sense of smell were more highly developed than everyone else's. What experiences might you have? How might your life change? What would you be able to smell? Write a story about a person with a very highly developed sense of smell.

41. Imagine yourself temporarily lost in a foreign country where you do not know the language. How do you manage to communicate? What might happen to you? Write a story about a day you might have spent lost in a foreign country without knowing the language.

42. Imagine a city project to have every school student do some hours of community service as a part of the required curriculum. What would you choose to do? What do you think it would be like? What people might you meet? What would you be doing to help? Write a story about a day of your community service.

43. Sometimes family members or friends embarrass you when other people are around. Think of some times this has happened to you. Think of what could happen. Write a story about some embarrassing incident you might have and how you coped with it.

44. Now and then you, without meaning to do so, break something that belongs to someone else. Think about what might be broken. Think about what might happen as a result. Now, write a story about accidentally breaking something that belonged to someone else and the story of what happened as a result.

45. One day your teacher must go home. Your teacher leaves, telling you that someone else will teach the class for the rest of the time. Who do you think will replace the teacher? What happens as a result? Write a story about a time your teacher had to go home, and someone else took over the class.

60 Persuasive Prompts for Elementary, Middle, and High Schools

1. Convince your parents to raise your allowance.

2. Should at least two years of foreign language classes be required for high-school graduation?

3. Should there be a dress code at your school?

4. Persuade your parents to listen to your favorite music.

5. Your principal has asked you to suggest one way of improving your school to make it a better place for students. Think about the changes that are needed at your school. Pick one change you feel would really make a difference, Write an essay to convince your principal that your idea is one that should be adopted.

6. Convince your teacher to read a favorite book of yours to the class.

7. Children watch too much television. Do you agree? Take a stand and support it. Convince your reader of your position.

8. Are part-time jobs for high school students a good thing or do they hinder getting an education? Take a stand.

9. Students are allowed to drop out of school at the age of 16. Should the state lower the school dropout age? Write an essay to support your view on the subject.

10. Should your school require uniforms? Convince your reader why or why not uniforms should or should not be required in your school.

11. Convince your parents to take you to a particular place.

12. Should gum chewing (use whatever is forbidden at your school) be allowed on the school campus?

13. Should community service be a requirement for graduation from high school?

14. Suppose you want a pet, and your parents are not sure you should have one. Think of the reasons for having a pet. Think of what you can say that would change your parents' minds. Write a paper to convince your parents to allow you to have a pet.

15. Persuade your mom to let you have your favorite food any time you want it.

16. Should the state legislature add ten days to the school year? Write to convince your reader of your side of the argument.

17. Should we do away with extra-curricular classes such as Art, P.E., and Music and go back to the basics, or are these classes necessary to a student's education?

18. Should homework be eliminated?

19. Considering the rights of the non-smokers, write an essay about whether smoking should or should not be permitted in public places. Convince your reader of your position.

20. Should students be allowed to drop out of school?

21. If you could make a suggestion to change the school dress code, what one suggestion would you make? Now write to convince your reader to adopt your suggestion.

22. Your teacher has asked for suggestions on a place to visit for a field trip. Where would you like to go? Convince your teacher to take the class there.

23. We have rules everywhere. Argue to support the need to change a rule or situation that affects you.

24. Vandalism is becoming a problem in today's society. Do you think teenagers who vandalize should pay fines or serve mandatory community service to help repair the damage? Write an essay to convince your reader of your position.

25. Should students hold after-school jobs? Convince your reader of your point of view.

> **NOTE:** *An attempt has been made to phrase the last thirty-five prompts as they might appear on the test. In many states, on the actual test, these prompts would be divided into three separate paragraphs. In the interest of space, I have omitted these separations and have written each prompt as one paragraph. Write them for your students the way they might appear on your state's writing tests.*

26. Parents, courts, and cities often impose curfews on teenagers. What do you think of curfews? Are they helpful in saving lives and keeping teenagers out of trouble, or are they just another insult to responsible teenagers? Think of some arguments to support your opinion. Now, write an essay to convince your reader your opinion regarding curfews for teenagers.

Alternative for younger students:

Most parents make their children come in before dark. What do you think of this? Does having to come home early help keep kids out of trouble or is it just another insult to responsible kids? Think of some arguments to support your opinion. Now, write an essay to convince your reader your opinion regarding requiring kids to be home before dark.

27. Many adults disagree whether sex education should be taught in the schools. What is your opinion on this matter? Should sex education be taught in the schools? Take a stand. Write an essay to convince your reader of your point of view on whether sex education should be taught in the schools or not.

Alternative for younger students

Some things are taught in school that students do not think should be taught. Think of one thing you are required to learn in school that you do not think should be included in the curriculum. Now, write an essay to convince your teachers to abandon that part of the curriculum.

28. The state writing assessment test puts pressure on students and their teachers. On the other hand, student writing all over the country has improved since this test has been implemented. What is your opinion on the matter? Should there be a state writing assessment test, or should this particular test be eliminated? Write an essay to convince your state of your opinion on whether there should (or should not) be a state writing assessment test.

29. Parents, schools, and society all impose rules, but schools especially have a set of rules that must be followed. Think of one school rule that you really dislike. Think of some arguments against having this rule at your school Now, write an essay to convince your principal and teachers to abandon this particular rule.

30. Universities require that an entering freshman must have taken at least two years of a foreign language in high school in order to be considered for admission. Some teachers and politicians think that high schools should require two years of a foreign language for graduation. What do you think of this possible requirement? Should high schools require two years of studying a foreign language for graduation? There are many arguments for and against this. What do you think? Write an essay to convince the powers-that-be whether or not two years of a foreign language should be a requirement for graduation from high school.

Alternative for younger students:

Research has shown that the younger you are, the easier it is to learn a foreign language. Should we start requiring that students begin taking a foreign language in elementary school? Take a stand and convince your reader of your opinion on requiring foreign language in elementary school.

31. Most families assign chores to the children (teenagers). Most children (teens) object to having these chores imposed upon them. What is your opinion? Do you think that children should have assigned chores to do at home, or do you think you have enough to do already? Write an essay to convince the adults in your family of your opinion regarding children (teenagers) being required to do chores at home.

32. There is a controversy (argument) going on in the country about requiring seat belts in school busses. What is your opinion? Should seat belts be required in all school busses? Write an essay to convince the powers-that-be of your opinion regarding the matter of whether seat belts should be required on school busses.

33. High schools do not offer all the elective courses that students would like to take. Think of an elective course you would like to take that your school does not offer at this time. Think of some reasons why you think this course should be offered. Now, write an essay to convince the administration at your high school to offer the course of your choice.

Alternative for younger students:

Schools do not offer all the elective courses like art and music that students would like to take. Think of a course you would like to take that your school does not offer at this time. Think of some reasons why you think this course should be offered. Now, write an essay to convince the principal of your school to offer the course of your choice.

34. In Europe the driving age is 18 because those governments feel that teens are not mature enough to handle the responsibility and the rules of driving in order to avoid accidents. In America, the driving age is still 16. Some people would like to raise the driving age in America to 18. What do you think? Should the driving age be raised to 18? Write an essay to convince the legislature of your position in the matter of raising the driving age to 18.

35 Most school systems have a separate school for pregnant teens to keep them away from other teens and to give them special classes to help them raise their babies. Do you think that pregnant teenagers should have to attend a special school, or do you think that they should be allowed to remain in their current school? Write an essay to convince your reader of your point of view. Should pregnant teenagers have to attend a special school?

Alternative for younger students:

Many school systems have special schools for students who misbehave all the time and disrupt the classroom so that little learning can take place. Do you think this is a good idea? What is your opinion? Write an essay to convince your school system of your point of view.

36. Many students object to the requirement of taking P.E., saying that it is not necessary. What do you think? Should Physical Education remain a required course at your school? Write an essay to convince your principal of your point of view.

NOTE: *You can substitute any unpopular course here. In my county, it would be Life Management Skills. Let your students suggest the course.*

37. American teenagers have argued that they drink anyway even though it is illegal for them to do so. Adults feel that they are too young to drink alcohol. Should the drinking age be lowered? What do you think about this? Think about some teens that you know. Think of some arguments to support your opinion. Now, write an essay to convince your reader of your opinion on whether the drinking age should be lowered or not.

38. In recent years, there has been much controversy over the previously solemn ritual of high school graduation. Students (and parents) at some graduation ceremonies have become rowdy and playful. What do you think of this? Should high school graduation continue to be the solemn occasion it has been in the past, or should students (and parents) be allowed to yell and "cut up" during the ceremony? Write an essay to convince your graduation committee of your opinion concerning the matter. Should graduation be a solemn occasion?

Alternative for younger students:

Some schools have graduation ceremonies in the fifth and eighth grade before students have completed their education. What do you think of this? Should students have graduation ceremonies before they finish all of their education or not? Think of some reasons to support your opinion. Now, write an essay to convince the reader of your point of view.

39. You hear the older generation complaining that they wished they had watched what they ate when they were younger so that they wouldn't have the health problems they have as older persons. What do you think of this? Should teens (children) watch what they eat? Should young people be health-conscious and eat healthily even though they have few health problems now? Write an essay to convince your reader of your point of view on whether or not children should watch their health through their choices in food.

40. Teachers and educational experts say that TV is rotting the mind of today's youth. They maintain that young people watch far too much television. Do you think this is true? Do you think that children watch too much television? Should parents restrict the number of hours their children watch? Write an essay to convince your parents of your point of view on this issue. Should parents limit your TV viewing?

41. Years ago, in some cities, there were separate public schools for boys and girls, especially at the high-school level. Boys went to one school and girls went to another near by, an entirely different school. Do you think this is a beneficial idea? Should boys and girls attend separate schools? Write an essay to persuade school officials whether or not they should separate boys and girls into different schools.

42. Most teens (children) complain that they get too little allowance. What do you think? Should you get more allowance? Think of some arguments to raise your allowance. Now, write an essay to the adults in your home to convince them to raise your allowance.

43. In many households where teens reside, possession of the family car is a conflict. How would you convince your parents to lend you the car? Think of some arguments you could use. Write an essay to convince the adults in your home to lend you the car whenever you want it.

Alternative for younger students:

In many households where there are children, there are many arguments over the use of the telephone. How would you convince your parents to get you a phone of your own? Think of some arguments you could use. Now, write an essay to convince your parents that you need a phone of your own.

> **NOTE:** *If some of your students have no phone in their home, perhaps they could convince parents to buy an outfit or handheld video game that their parents could afford.*

44. Students complain about having too much homework. Do you think this is true? Do your teachers assign too much homework, or do they not give you enough for you to learn the subjects? Write an essay to convince your teachers either to give you more or less homework.

45. Test scores show that the United States is educationally behind other developed countries in Europe and Asia. We need to take a course of action to improve our education. Some think that the school year should be extended year round with only short breaks between semesters. Others think it would not help. What do you think? Write an essay to persuade the reader of your opinion on the matter. Should the school year be lengthened?

46. Many people think that smoking is a dangerous habit that kills many from lung cancer. They think that cigarette smoking is not only dangerous for the people who smoke, but also for others around them. They think that the tobacco companies lure young people into smoking (convince young people to smoke) with their clever advertisements. Do you think that smoking should be made illegal? Do you think that no one should be allowed to smoke at all? Or, do you think that the choice of smoking should be up to the individual person? What is your opinion? Take a stand. Should all smoking be banned and made illegal? Write an essay to convince the reader of your point of view.

47. In the 1920s it was illegal to sell or to drink alcohol. Today alcohol still causes many problems for the people who drink and for their families. There are also many deaths caused by people (teens) who drink and drive. Should alcohol be made illegal again? Would making it illegal solve some problems, or would it impinge (limit) the rights of adults to do what they want to do? What do you think? Should the sale and drinking of alcohol again be made illegal? Write an essay to convince the reader of your point of view.

48. Many people are convinced that violence on TV influences children and teens to be violent in real life. Do you think that this is true? Do you think that the violence on TV is responsible for increased violence among today's youth? Take a stand on this issue and write an essay to convince your reader of your position on whether TV causes violence in real life.

49. Some schools in the United States are requiring that students volunteer for several hours each semester to help on a community problem. What do you think? Is this a good idea? Will it help solve some of the problems in your community? Write an essay to persuade your reader of your point of view on whether students should be required to volunteer for several hours each semester to help on a community problem.

50. School dress codes often cause conflict among students and teachers. If you were on a committee of teachers and students to set the dress code at your school, what one item of your dress code would you argue to allow students to wear? How would you convince your fellow committee members to accept your idea to allow students to wear this item? Now, write an essay to convince your fellow dress-code committee members that the clothing item you chose should be allowed at your school.

> **NOTE:** *Conversely, (to be contrary) you could have a prompt to argue one item of clothing that should not be allowed at your school.*

51. Your local TV station is going to hire a student reporter for the evening news program, and you would like the job. Think about your local evening news program and why you should be chosen as the student reporter. Now write an essay to convince your local TV station to hire you as their student reporter.

52. The drama teacher is selecting students to act in a play about famous people. Think of yourself and some of your friends. Think who would be best suited to act in such a play and why they would be good at it. Now write an essay to convince the drama teacher to use that person in the play.

53. A national organization is honoring a teacher. Who should that teacher be? Think of some of the excellent teachers you have had in the past or have this year. Pick one whom you think should be honored by this award. Think of some reasons why you picked this teacher. Now write an essay to convince the national organization to honor the teacher you picked.

54. The School Advisory Council has money to spend in one of the following ways: improving the cafeteria, buying computers, getting interesting speakers for assemblies, or taking field trips. Pick one of these choices and think why you chose it over the others. Now write an essay to convince the School Advisory Council why they should spend their money on the choice you suggest.

55. The City Council wants a teen as a member to represent your age group. Think of yourself and the teens you know. Who would make an excellent representative on the City Council? Think of some reasons why you chose this person. Now write an essay to convince the City Council to select your choice.

56. Imagine that your school does not have a school newspaper. Your principal wants to begin one. Is a school newspaper a good idea? What do you think? Write an essay to convince your principal of your point of view.

57. A good friend of yours is thinking of moving to your town. Think of some attributes of your town that would appeal to your friend. Now write an essay to convince your friend to move to your town.

58. Imagine that you had a friend who ate only junk food, and you know that this is not good for him or her. Think of some reasons why eating junk foods is not good for people. Now write an essay to convince your friend that eating healthy foods is a good idea.

59. A movie director is looking for teens to act in a movie that will be set in your town. Think of yourself and all the teens you know. Who would you choose to act in this movie? Think why you would choose this person. Write an essay to convince the movie director of your choice.

60. If your school is going to grant your grade level one privilege that the other grades in your school will not have, what should that privilege be? Think of one privilege that you would like to have that you do not have now. Think why your class should be granted this privilege. Write an essay to convince the administrators of your school to grant this privilege to your class for the rest of the year.

STEP FOUR

Teach Students to Be Able to Write from a Point of View Other Than Their Own (Expository/Clarification and Persuasive/Point of View) and Encourage Enthusiasm and Passion (Narrative, Descriptive, Expository/Clarification, and Persuasive)

1. Teach Your Students the Following by Any Means Possible

- How to write from a point of view other than their own.

  Suggestion — Have students cluster and write same prompt from several different angles. You can tell them which angle.

  Examples:

  Prompt — "Favorite Season" — Ask students to write two essays, on two different seasons.

  Prompt — "Uniforms, Yes or No?" — Ask students to write two essays, one "yes" and one "no."

- How to take a true story and amplify it with fiction.

  Suggestion — Have students embellish true stories (and prompts) orally and then in writing.

- Teach students to write with *passion* and *flair*.

Suggestions —

a) Read them selections written with passion and flair.

b) Be passionate yourself about writing.

c) Become a Six God or Goddess and be very dramatic. Spread "Magic Six Dust" liberally and pass out "Magic Six Mints."

d) Encourage passion in writing and note it when students demonstrate it.

e) Hold a pep rally for writing.

- Make students familiar with a plethora of superlative vocabulary words.

Suggestions —

a) Use *Caught'yas* daily and use the vocabulary words frequently with your students.

b) Encourage students to use new words in their writing. (Give extra credit.)

c) Put vocabulary words (found in reading selections or from students) on the board.

d) Hold Dictionary Days (explained in **Section 4**)

- Teach students a variety of quotations they can call upon when needed.

Suggestions —

a) Put a quote of the week on the board and invite students to bring in their favorite quotes to use in subsequent weeks. Refer to them frequently. Repeat them daily.

b) Share your own favorite quotes.

2. Persuasive and Expository/ Clarification Topics

- ### Rationale for Teaching Students to Write What They Can Support

This is an extremely important part of high scores, especially on the seventh/eighth- and tenth-grade tests which include persuasive essays in almost every state that requires a writing assessment test. It is a given that most students will not like the topic they are assigned. Expository/Clarification and persuasive essays are particularly bad in this respect because students tend to "knee jerk" their answers to such a prompt without thinking whether or not they can adequately support it. They must learn to take whichever side of a topic they can support the best, **whether or not it expresses their own personal opinion!**

A prime example was the 1993 eighth-grade persuasive topic in my state. It asked students to argue whether the school year should be extended by ten days. Not surprisingly, an overwhelming number of students tried to argue against extending the year. In discussions with eighth graders after the test, most conceded that better arguments, however, could have been more easily found to support the other point of view, especially since the topic suggested extending the school year by only ten days.

That year the persuasive scores were low, probably due to the fact that most students who got that topic (including mine) wrote what they felt, not what they had persuasive arguments to support.

The following year a similar topic was given, but this time my students were ready to take either side of the argument before they wrote. In fact, many students confided to me after the test that they heartily disagreed with what they had written but had taken the point of view that they could better support with more convincing arguments. My students' scores on the persuasive essay rose considerably that year.

The problem is also similar for expository/ clarification essays. It is a fact of life, I think, that students will detest the prompt they get on the test and not wish to "waste their time writing about it." I warn my students of this, repeating this homily many times so that, hopefully, on the day of the test, they will say to themselves, "Gee, this isn't such a bad topic." They just have to learn to "keep their cool" and write away! Read on for a few ideas about how to train your students to take an "unpopular" stand.

- ### Procedure to Teach Students to Argue Both Sides

When students are comfortable clustering, writing, and scoring, it is time to introduce the concept of trying both sides of an issue or topic. Begin by having the class as a whole come up with arguments to support an unpopular topic, such as to increase homework or lengthen the school year, or require uniforms, etc. Write the arguments on the board. Cluster the other side as well in order to show students that the important thing is not **which** side they take but that they write the topic they can support best, whether they agree with it or not.

After clustering a few times as a whole class, give students another unpopular topic. (Ask the students to suggest some ideas.) Then divide the students into groups of four and assign half of the groups to find support for the unpopular side and the other half to find support for the popular one. Discuss the results. It is a good idea to do this several times so that all students experience both sides.

Next, assign another topic, hand out two of the **Essay Plan Form** sheets and have students, individually this time, plan both sides of the topic. Discuss the results as a class. It might be a good idea to time your students as they plan since you don't want them to get into the habit of spending too much time planning. Ten minutes per side of the topic should be sufficient. At this point, students are **not** writing the essays. If you have enough transparencies, have students put their plans on them and share them, using the overhead projector. It helps students to see their peers' plans.

Finally, assign prompts and tell students which side to take. This time, they are to plan **and write** essays. Vary the tack. Sometimes make them write the unpopular opinion and other times make them argue the side they, themselves, would probably naturally choose.

Keep stressing that no one except the persons who score their essays will know what they write on the actual test. These are scored by people who do not know them or their school. (One year I think ours were even sent out of state.) It is the test score that is important, not which point of view they select to support.

3. Encourage Passion in Narrative, Descriptive, Expository/Clarification, and Persuasive Topics

No essay or story is going to be interesting unless it is written with passion and enthusiasm. If you find that your students lack enthusiasm or cannot passionately get into their essays (this is especially true at the high-school level), a pep rally a day or two before the test is in order! Have students sit on the floor with you and talk about things that they could write passionately about. Have them visualize feeling strongly enough about the topic to be able to write passionately. Hold a real pep rally. After all, they have them for sports...

It is good to start early, encouraging students to write with passion (sounding a bit enthusiastic yourself at the thought). I like to ask my students after each practice, "Now, who wrote that last essay with passion? Who threw his/her soul into the paper?" A few hands of your boldest students invariably go up (since this is a good thing to have done). You can then continue the brief discussion about how they felt as they wrote.

Reading examples of obviously passionately written essays and narratives to the class also can help raise enthusiasm for otherwise rather dull-sounding efforts. Good examples of peer writing efforts often can spark better writing.

My teaching partner, Tim McShane, stresses "passion in writing" to his students on a daily basis. His students obviously follow his advice since they also score well on the state writing assessment. His theory is that without passion, there is no really good writing. I agree. The high scores of **5.5** and **6** are awarded only to those whose papers followed the few mandatory guidelines and demonstrate verve and passion for the subject.

4. Fun Ways to Learn and Retain Great Vocabulary

- **Use *Caught'yas***

    Teach the conventions using *Caught'yas* (Kiester 1990, 1993, 1998, 2000). Each day's *Caught'ya* sentences contain at least one great vocabulary word, usually more. Teach them. Use them in your speech regularly. Make your students keep a vocabulary notebook in which they put the daily vocabulary word. Challenge your students to use these words in their writing and give extra credit if they box them (so that you easily can see them) and use them correctly.

- **Hold Dictionary Days**

    This is a simple activity that works incredibly well to put great vocabulary words into your students' minds so permanently that they use them in their writing. My students beg to have frequent "Dictionary Days" because they enjoy them so much! My teaching partners, who do not hold "Dictionary Days," swear that *their* students learn the words by osmosis! Here's how this activity works.

    A. Give your students a vocabulary list (any list of great words will do). Since I link writing and vocabulary to works of literature, I use the list of words that I find in the book we currently are reading and type a copy of them for my students to learn.

B. After students look up the meaning and part of speech of all the words on the list (individually or in groups), ask each student to pick out one word they would like to teach to their peers. Write down each student's word in your gradebook as you do not wish to have two students choose the same word. (This year I had two students fight over the word "puerile." Students really get into this activity with a passion.)

C. A few days before "Dictionary Day," ask students to plan how they will teach their word and what they will wear to illustrate its meaning. It is a good idea to ask them to do this in writing. Students must think of a clever way to teach the meaning of their word so that their peers will remember it. They must also figure out a way to illustrate the word in their dress and make a large card with the word printed in large letters.

A good example would be how one of my students dressed for "puerile" this year. She wore her hair in pigtails, dressed like a small child, acted very childish, and carried a borrowed doll. Across her chest in big letters blazed the word "puerile." Another imaginative student cut his parents' bushes and draped himself in them. The word he put on his green cap in big letters was "bracken," but he could have used "foliage." The student who picked "carnage" used make-up to draw bloody cuts across her face. Another carried a placard proclaiming the end of the world and the word "apocalyptic." The child who taught "flabbergasted" made her hair stand on end in large clumps and wore a surprised expression on her face all day. The usually talkative student who chose the word "mute" did not say a word all day and communicated by way of note! You will be amazed how creative your students get. These were just a few of the examples of what students come up with on "Dictionary Day."

D. On the designated day, students come to school dressed to illustrate the meaning of their word and prominently display the actual word somewhere on their person so all can see it clearly. They also carry a piece of paper (or tape one to their back) on which they have numbered from one to forty (or more if you wish). They

must wear their word all day and teach it to, as well as get the signatures of, students I have in any of my classes during the day. They teach their word and get signatures at lunch, in between classes, and in my classroom that day. We also spend the entire class period teaching words and getting signatures.

It is a good idea to warn your colleagues in advance. Since I teach middle school, and my students change classes, my fellow teachers jump into the spirit of the day and use in their own parlance the words that they see emblazoned on my students' bodies. The Dean even gets into the activity at lunch and points out the words and definitions of particularly creative children. All in all, it is a fun day for all, and everyone learns new words.

E. I give grades for creativity (a "C" if I had to help the child make his costume the morning of "Dictionary Day"), for getting the required number of signatures, and then a test grade. For the latter, I simply walk around the room the day following "Dictionary Day," lists in hand, and ask students who signed a sheet the meaning of that word. I ask three students per list. If all three know the meaning, the student to whom the list belongs gets an "A." The average test grade is an "A+."

• **Making Games to Play**

Using the words from any vocabulary list you provide, ask students to invent a game to teach the word. Students can work in pairs to make their games. They may invent new games or use an old game board (like "Candyland") for their game. The key is that before a player is allowed to move, he/she must draw a card with a vocabulary word on it and tell the definition. The makers of the game must provide a master list with the words and definitions, so that whoever is playing the game can check to see if he/she is correct. The maker(s) of each game also must include directions.

It is a good idea to spend two to three class periods playing the games. Students like to play each other's games as well as their own.

- **Old-fashioned "Vocabulary Bees"**

Instead of a spelling bee, hold a "Vocabulary Bee"! Give students a list of words, ask them to make flash cards, writing the meaning and part of speech on one side and the word on the other. Give your students a day to drill each other. Then hold the "Vocabulary Bee." In the spirit of the competition, your students will learn the meaning of a plethora of words.

- **Circle of Meanings**

A. Divide your students into groups of ten or twelve (no more than three groups in the class). Each group picks a name, a leader, a recorder, a scorekeeper, and a word keeper.

B. Hand each group the same list of juicy vocabulary words (at least 50 words on the list).

C. Ask each group to look up the meaning and part of speech of the words and then drill each other until they "learn" them. They then pick ten of the words they want to learn "really well." The group studies these words. You will have to check each group's words to make sure that there are few or no repetitions of words.

D. Now they are ready to play the game. Set up three desks in front of your room. Each group's leader brings the list of ten words and meanings his or her group chose and sits at one of the desks. I like to post each group's name on the desk.

E. The leaders ask students in other groups, in turn, to define a given word. If the chosen student cannot give the correct meaning, his/her team loses a point and the group that asked the word asks the second group. If the student in this latter group does not know the answer, his/her group loses a point and the word goes to the group of the leader who asked the word. If the chosen member of the leader's group cannot correctly give the meaning of the word, his/her team loses two points! Play progresses with a point given for each correct answer until all the words have been asked. It is a good idea to ask leaders to have back-up words in case students really get into this or you goofed when checking the ten words picked, and there is duplication.

F. It is very important to keep this game fair and not let your students constantly pick on the weakest learners in the class who still may not know the meanings. In order to instill perfect fairness into the game, I give a copy of my seating chart to every student. As a student is called upon to give a definition, everyone puts a check by that student's name. No leader may call on that student again until all the members of his/her group have been called on to supply a definition. We sometimes play until each student in the class (including the leaders) has been called on at least twice.

5. Writer's Pizzazz

The following pages contain a partial list of the pizzazz and flair that writers use to keep their readers hooked and interested. Some are simple to teach, and others will require much practice on the part of your students in order to implement correctly and effectively in their writing. These little tricks put passion and flair into writing and earn young writers the highest scores on the writing assessment tests.

You may copy the following two pages to use with your students however you wish. I suggest that you introduce some of these devices through the use of my *Caught'yas*, through the vocabulary games listed above, through reading examples of literature, and through practice.

Conclusion

If you and your students have followed the four steps explained in this book, they will be on their way to higher scores on your state writing assessment test. If nothing else, the frequent writing practice, the exposure to many writing ideas, and the constant encouragement of an enthusiastic teacher will boost the writing of your poorest producers and incite your best writers to soar! The end result will be better writing fluency for all, and that, of course, is the true goal.

Writers' "PIZZAZZ" Used to Dazzle the Reader

anecdote — A story within a story to catch the reader's fancy.

catchy title — A title that creates interest or arouses curiosity.

dialogue — This can come in many forms, with or without a tag. It can be repartée (quick and witty), in vernacular (the language of the people), or just an ordinary conversation.

figurative language — These are some of the most common ones.
    personification (The leaves danced in the wind.)
    similes (The leaves moved like dancers.)
    metaphor (The green ballerinas danced in the wind.)
    alliteration (The lovely leaves leapt from their lofty perch)
    onomatopoeia ("**Cough, cough**" spluttered the sick child.)
    oxymoron — words put together that have opposite meanings such as *jumbo shrimp*

foreign language — If a writer knows a bit of a foreign language, a commonly known phrase for example, like *Bonjour,* can be very effective.

grabber or hook — This is a way of introducing an essay or story that wakes up the reader, grabs his/her attention, and makes him/her want to read more. A grabber can be in the form of a question, a quick dialogue of some sort (usually untagged), onomatopoeia, a quote, etc.

humor — This can be a witty phrase, a short joke, a funny incident that is related to the story or essay, anything that would amuse the reader.

literary allusion — Referring to commonly known books is always effective.

nitty-gritty detail — Detail can come in many forms, but no broad statement (for example: "I have a nice house") should be made without being followed by detail that lets you know about what is in the statement. This can be in the form of a brief story, a description, an anecdote, a list of attributes, etc.

painting word pictures — Strong, active verbs evoke vivid, descriptions that paint pictures in words pictures so clear that the reader has no trouble imaging it in his/her mind. Victor Hugo and Dickens were masters of this technique.

quotes — The use of quotes whether from the author, from people the author knows, or from well-known people is always a good way to add pizzaz. "To be or not to be, that is the question." — Shakespeare

sensory words — These are words that elucidate writing like, "The *tangy* smell of *pungent* salsa permeated the room.

"showing, not telling" writing — This is a technique used to avoid vague statements like "The girl was frightened." Instead, a frightened girl is "shown" to the reader. For example: "The frightened girl *quivered* as her knees *knocked* together, her throat *closed up*, and her mouth *lost* all moisture. She could not even *scream* her terror."

sound words — Sound words can mimic any sound you hear. For example, *toot toot* for the sound of a tugboat or *thbbbth* for a "raspberry." These also are called *onomatopoeia.*

strong, active verbs — These verbs say "The cat *sprawled* in the chair." rather than "The cat was in the chair."

threading a theme throughout — This would be like the song that identifies the dwarves in "Snow White" or the web in *Charlotte's Web* that is mentioned on almost every page.

unusual transitions — See **Useful Devices** for examples "$100" vocabulary words - Frequent use of august vocabulary words shows mastery of language.

zinger — This is an ending that zings the reader so that he/she is surprised, provoked to think, or made to laugh or cry.

Fifty-three Examples for Scoring Practice

Introduction to Examples

On the following pages are five sets of examples, one set from the average, heterogeneous fourth-grade class of Amy Rollo at Littlewood Elementary School, Gainesville, Florida, two more sets from eighth-grade language arts classes (one regular and one advanced) at Westwood Middle School, Gainesville, Florida, another set from a regular tenth-grade English class of Jim Owens at Gainesville High School, and a set from seventh graders of Renée Trufant at Brevard Middle School in Brevard, North Carolina. The papers were typed *basically as the students wrote them*, egregious spelling errors and all. I did slightly doctor one or two of the Florida papers by adding other students' examples to make a composite or by deleting parts so that the papers more clearly exemplified each of the scores. After all, the purpose of these examples is to give you and your students practice scoring and to show typical examples of each type of score, not to show you what a few students can write on a given day. The last four sets of examples are scored on a LOW, MEDIUM, HIGH scale. The first set (from North Carolina) are scored on a scale of 1 to 4 and were not changed in any way since they were officially scored.

Amy, Jim, Renée, and I had been working very diligently with our students to ensure good scores on our state's writing assessment. Thus, when reading through sets of papers from class after class to find examples for this book, I discovered that finding papers with the lowest scores was difficult. Our students had learned well. Most of the papers I read were in the **medium** range with a fair number of **HIGHS**, but only a handful of papers with a really low score or below. I put the papers into five sets, one for fourth, two for eighth, one for tenth, and one for seventh.

The first set of examples are descriptive. There are eleven of them. They were written by Renée Trufant's seventh graders and were actually scored by the state of North Carolina. The topic is **"Describe a place where you go to have fun."**

The second and third sets of examples are expository/clarification topics written by eighth graders. The first expository topic is **"What book would you recommend that the whole class read? Give reasons why you recommend this book."** The second set of eighth-grade examples also respond to a totally expository topic: **"If your principal asked you to head a committee to improve the lunchroom conditions, what would you suggest?"** Since the set that came from my classroom (the "Lunchroom") are from students I no longer teach, I have long since forgotten which student wrote which essay. Most of the other set (the "Book"), in fact, were given to me by Mary Ann Coxe, head of English for Alachua County, Florida. She had collected them from various eighth-grade teachers around the county and given them to eighth-grade teachers to use as a tool in learning how to score the state writing assessment. For the last few years I have been using both sets of these examples with my students as I teach them to score expository/clarification essays. I hope you find them useful. There are seven papers (one for each score) for each topic, fourteen papers in all.

The fourth set of examples was written by fourth graders in response to a narrative topic. **"Every day you pass a door. It is always locked. One day, as you pass, you notice that the door is open. You step inside. Write a story about what was on the other side of the door."**

Amy gave this prompt to her students right after the test in February so they are a fairly accurate representative of how her students performed on the test. I have included two examples of each score from **high** to **unscorable** in order to give you plenty of them to peruse.

The last set of examples was written by Jim Owen's regular (as opposed to Honors) tenth graders. The topic was persuasive: **"Should Community Service be a requirement for high-school graduation?"** I deliberately used a regular high school class because in a set of essays from an Honors Class, I would not have found an example of a very low score. Once again, I have included two examples of each possible score, a total of fourteen papers in this set.

No matter what grade level you teach, you can use *all* of these examples to teach scoring to your students. I have found that the quality of most of the examples are surprisingly similar from grade to grade. The good ones are good, and the poor ones are poor. The poor fourth-grade samples are less sophisticated but no worse than the poor eighth-and tenth-grade ones. Similar spelling and grammatical errors occur in all three grades. In fact, one of the examples in the tenth-grade set is from a student I had taught in the eighth grade. He doggedly still is making some of the same spelling errors he did two years ago.

Please note that after each set of examples you will find a section with the scores for each paper in the set and a brief reason for each score. I have organized it in this fashion to make it easier for you to copy the examples without copying the scores.

To make it more realistic for you, I have mixed up the order of the examples so that, for instance, Example #1 in a set could be a **LOW** and Example #2 could be a **HIGH**. After you have scored each example, you can match the example numbers to find out the score that my colleagues and I assigned each paper. Do not be dismayed if you disagree with us. Judges do disagree. That is why there are split scores (like **4.5** on a 1-6 point scale) when the writing assessment results come back — one judge gave the paper one score and the second judge gave it a score lower or higher. If you are off by a level, go back to **Step 2** and read once more the required elements of each score.

1. Descriptive Examples

TOPIC: "Describe a place where you go to have fun so that your reader can picture it."

NOTE: These particular examples actually were scored by the official scorers of the State of North Carolina. North Carolina very kindly sends the papers with the scores attached back to the teachers so that the papers (as well as the scores) can be filed in student folders, students can have their memory refreshed as to what they wrote to receive the score they earned, and teachers can copy some of the essays (without the names on them) and use these examples with future students to practice scoring.

NOTE ALSO: North Carolina requires that descriptions be mostly visual and scores on a scale of **1** to **4**. This score does not include the conventions. These are scored separately. If your state uses a rubric of **1** to **5** or **1** to **6**, you easily can translate a **1** to a low score, a **2** to a low to medium score, a **3** to a medium score, and a **4** to a high score. These papers came from a school which has excellent teachers and whose students rarely earn less than a **1.5**. Thus, that is the lowest score among the following examples.

Sample Set #1
Descriptive — "A Place to Have Fun"

Example #1

Chirp, chirp, those are just some of the wonderful sounds that you hear at a fun place like the beach.

At the beach you can her the soothing sounds of the ocean waves hitting the ocean floor. When it is dark and silent outside, you can hear the ocean banging on the shore, it sounds like someone is shooting a rifle. You will be awoken by the yelling and screaming of kids on the beach. It sounds like you are at a big carnival. If you look out of your hotel window you can see all kinds of people running everywhere. Some are even playing vollyball or tennis but those aren't all the things you can do on a hot windy day at the beach. There are even sounds of birds singing. Birds are all different colors there like rainbow's floating high in the windy sky. The birds eat bread and seeds off of the dark brown sand.

The sand is rough like sandpaper, when you run on it with just you're bare feet. The seashells make it hard to walk on in some places. Beneath you're feet the sand feels cold from the ocean water, you can feel the sand comeing up between you're tired little toes. When you walk on the sand at night you have to watch out for the night crawlers, such as little birds, snails, and pincher's. If you stand on the sand close to the water it feels like you're flouting for a second.

The ocean floor is sometimes rough because of the jagged shells and rocks. If you go further out you can feel the smooth sinsation of the soft and smushy ocean floor. If you watch you can see big white looking fish jump out of the water, like something down there is going to eat them. There is sometimes dolphines further out in the ocean that jump up and scwigle like they've never scwigled before. The ocean tastes like someone just poored five million gallons of salt in the water. The ocean fills the hole air with the fragrinte of salt.

If you have never been to the beach you might want to think about going. It is a wonderful place to be and have fun at. If everyone who go's to the beach likes it I know you will.

Sample Set #1
Descriptive — "A Place to Have Fun"

Example #2

Aah, hey watch it, swish! These are all sounds you would hear if you went to Franklin Park. At Franklin there's a slide, merry-go-round, Jungle Jym.

In front of you when you first go to Franklin is the slide. The slide has a nice cool feeling on a hot summer day. The slide it's self is silver. But the ladder to climb up is a old orange-red color. The "waiting area" is a nice deep blue that makes you feel like going swimming. And the poles to the side are like royal blue hands lightly touching the ground. Yet the slide is so high up that it seems as if you could touch the baby blue cloudless sky. To your right though is the merry-go-round.

I like the merry-go-round the best (Ol' Rusty). Ol' Rusty he's the fast thing you have ever set on (if you've never been on a roller coster) and on him it seems as if you could go on forever and ever. I like Ol' Rusty's wooden seats they're about the color of a weather washed board. And the rust on the medal makes you just want to sit not spin. I love Ol' Rusty. I just wouldn't suggest anyone with a weak stomach to go on or you wouldn't have to worry about staying there much longer. Many people sit were Ol' Rusty's the fastest his middle. To the far back of the park is Jungle Gym.

Now Jungle Gym, he can be one of the most frustrating things you have ever seen. All the up's and downs. But hey he's eye catching. Jungle Gym has a red latter, blue latter, orange latter. Boy I even think he's got a green one. I think he's got five or six latters. He is very peculiar of who gets one him. If he don't like the child Gym will have him lost in a second. But if he like the child he'll let him get to the pole to slide down with no problem's at all. The pole is at the end of the Jungle Gym and is rainbow colored.

Franklin Park is one of the most exiting places to ever be but on the earth. From slides, to merry-go-rounds, and even a Jungle Gym.

Sample Set #1
Descriptive — "A Place to Have Fun"

Example #3

Have you ever been to a pulcurtudinous park that had a pool, a snack bar, and a ice cream truck that promenetly came at 3:32 p.m. Well I have and I want to describe it to you so you can understand it better.

Click, Clat, Click, Clat, Click, that's what you will hear about 12:00 pm if your wating in line at Franklin Park. As soon as you walk in the door you see a woman sitting in a chair behind glass saying one dollar kids, two dollar's adults. To your imediet left is the boy's bathroom. And to your imediet right is the girl's bathroom. The room the woman is in is a square room, you can walk all the way around it. On the other side of the woman is a snack bar it has Reesies, rice cryspy treet's, Snickers, Peps, Mountain Dew, life Savers, and Crunch Bars.

Blue water, cement suroandings, life gourd stands is what you will find if you go strait away from the snack Bar. It is and outside Pool about 9 ft deep in the deep end and about 3 ft deep in the shallow end. It has a rope with flotaition devices on it in the middle of the Pool. The Pool is surounded By a 6 foot tall fence.

About 3:32 pm every day you hear ding, ping, tong, and that meens the ice cream truck is coming so every body gets there money and rushes up the steps, out the door to catch the ice cream man. "Stop" the kids scream, and the ice cream man stops. Everyone is saying I want chocolate, I want strawberry. I want vanilia. And the ice cream man say's o'kay, o'kay one at a time, so everybody gets there ice cream and goe's back to the Pool to get cooled of agian.

In conclusion, go to Franklin Park to have the best time of your life in just one day.

Sample Set #1
Descriptive — "A Place to Have Fun"

Example #4

Splash! Many kids jump into the enormous lake at the Southside Park. Many people come here to have a great time. Some people come to swim in the lake, others to work out in the gym. People even come to go in the woods. All of the places are fun.

The lake is a great place to have fun. A whole lot of people can come to swim because the beautiful lake is about the size of three football fields. Standing from the fifty docks where the boats are boarded, you can see the ground because the water is so clean and clear. Across the lake from the docks there is a rope swing that is azure blue and brings you high into the air. About 20 feet away from the swing there is a rock that has water gushing over it. It is great to slide down into the chilling water. Above the rock is a tiny tree house that has a zip line trailing out of the house in the sky. The crimson sip line connects to a huge tree in the woods. The lake is a good reason to come to Southside Park.

As you walk into the woods, the oak trees tower over you. You may even see a doe prance across the path. the path is actually a 4-wheeling path. The dirt is always flying everywhere. At the end of the path there are horse stables. The path is also used for horseback riding. In the distance, between the oak trees, there is a wild creek. It glides smoothly over the rocks. Down stream a little there is a cabin. The cabin is in usually empty. Some people go in there to get away from everyone. Everyone loves the woods.

Out of the woods and across from the lake there is a gym. It is very noticable because the outside is neon yellow. The building is a dome and the roof is completly glass. Inside the gym there is a room for weight lifting. Every machine that is for building strength is there. Across the hall there is a basketball court. Many people come in to play games and build strength. If you might need a snack, there is a Subway down the hall. Beside the Subway there is a sauna. Many people go in there to get hot. A lot of people go into the gym to have fun also.

Many people come to Southside Park to have the time of their lives. I believe that it is a great way to have fun. You can go swimming, work out in the gym or go for a hike in the woods.

Sample Set #1
Descriptive — "A Place to Have Fun"

Example #5

Smash-Clash-Whing-Boom! Do you hear that? That's the sound of people having fun. To have fun you can go to a club, theampark, and the mountains.

My first reason is to go to a club. People go to clubs to dance around with people, hang out with friends, and to meet new people. People like to hang out with their friends at clubs because it's fun. You have the music, drinks, and people, so you can hang out with your friends and other people to. While your in the club with the music blasting, hangin out, you can also meet new people who could like things that you like to.

Second you can go to a theampark and have fun there too. You can go swimming, you can hang out, you can also do thing that you've never done before. For example you can go down a big slide in a innertube, slide down huge water slides, float down a river, go on a roller coaster, go on a big ship that flips around in circles. In a theampark you can hang out with friends and do every thing that I listed.

My final reason is that you can also go to the mountains and have fun. In the mountains you can go mountain climbing with family and friends, you can go bike riding on a mountain bike, and you can also go river rafting. All of these are fun. You can go river rafting on a big raft, you can go biking on a trail in the mountains, and you can go mountain climbin on a lot of mountains with a harness and rope. Taking a trip to the mountains is a lot of fun and you can spend that fun time with who ever you want to spend it with.

Now if you ever think about going some where to have fun and you go to a club, theampark, or the mountains, just thing of all the things I've said and have fun.

Sample Set #1
Descriptive — "A Place to Have Fun"

Example #6

Little kids running wild, people on the basketball court waiting to get a game going, runners working hard to get in shape, all of these things take place at one of the most fun places I know. The park. There are all kinds of activities, many different happy sounds, and beautiful sights everywhere in the park that make it a really cool place be.

When you first arrive at the park, the first thing you notice are all of the different sounds surrounding you. Many birds fly all around you, each singing a different beautiful song. Then you hear the happy squeals that the little kids make as their parents push them in the swing, or as they shoot down the slides. Splash! The next sound you hear are people cooling off by taking a dive into the refreshing pool with its blue crystal water. Another sound seems to be getting closer. It's the sound of a group of people's quickly moving feet racing around the park. Next, you hear the bouncing of basketballs and you hear the excitement of the players as they score a point. The sound of cars coming to pick up or let off their kids, is never far away. Now you hear the sounds of people playing music to get them pumped up for their day at the park. Wherever you are in the park, their are always many unique sounds to be heard.

After you've engulfed all of the sounds around the park, you can start to check out all of the fun things people are taking part in. To begin with, there are all different types of sports being played. Adults and children enjoy biking or running around the park. Basketball is also very popular. Ten or fifteen people of all ages run up and down the court trying to prove that their the best. Next you see a ball fly through the air and realize many people are playing football. As you progress through the park you see boys and girls in their bathing suits getting ready to take a dip in the cold refreshing pool. Some people don't prefer activities, and you can see many lounge on the grass as they come just to relax and hang out with friends.

The scenery at the park is gorgious. There are so many different plants and trees and many other exciting things to see. To begin with, you notice all of the trees and flowers of lots of different colors that spark up the park's looks. There are dogwoods just blossoming and little maple trees that have been freshly planted. Tall oak trees provide shade for people. Next are the flowers. Lilyies line the outside of the park.

So, in conclusion, the park is the most fun and exciting place I know. If you're ever bored, or tired of the same old thing, go to the park and embark on a exciting, and exhilerating day.

Sample Set #1
Descriptive — "A Place to Have Fun"

Example #7

I am going to tell you a little bit about where people go to have fun. Read along and I will tell you.

The first place I decided where people should go to have fun is the museum. the museum is a place where you can learn about and explore many different ancient creatures that lived long ago. For example dinosaurs romed the earth thousands of years ago. The other creature you can learn about is how big was the tranisurous. The basic reason why you would want to go to the museum is because you can explore the adventures of the cavemen or you can find out how people realy existed on earth. The last but certainly not the least thing to explore is the aquarium things like the octopus. You could find out how the octopus realy did get those suction cups under his tentacles.

See so it as worth reading after all you probably want to go to the museum now dont you I know I do.

Sample Set #1
Descriptive — "A Place to Have Fun"

Example #8

The most fun place in the world to me is the Carnival. Because of all the rides, games, and shows there. As you continue reading I'll explain why.

When you first get there all you can see is rides. Left to right, right to left everywhere. The rides go around and around, upside down even sideways. With lights tons of lights piled on each ride so that each one glows in it's own special way. As the lights of blueberry blue, strawberry red, buttercup yellow, firey orange, and even violet purple swirl and twirl all around the rides making each and every ride look like a rainbow wrapped around them.

Second of all is the games. Games with spectacular prizes for each one. One of the most intriguing parts about the games to me is the people inside each one finding a different way to attract people like changing their voices but usually bigger prizes turn people on. Prizes like clover green giant stuff teddy bears fire truck red stuffed dogs. I even like the ones where you win real animals like gold fish or bunny rabbits.

Last but not least is the shows. Each one eye catching an pulchritudinous in it's own way. Shows like where people swallow fire. Amazing musicians, or even famous tatooed people. Each little show is great not a single one in the whole Carnival is dull or boring. Because if you watch then you would realize how unique and special each one makes the carnival look.

These few details are what makes the carnival look and be the most fun place in the world to me.

Sample Set #1
Descriptive — "A Place to Have Fun"

Example #9

There are many places where people go to have fun, but the one that is the best is Champion Park. The pool, basketball courts, and of course play ground all make it a fantastic place to enjoy yourself.

As you pull up to this park you will audamatcly see the basketball courts. They are black as night with baby blue lines that show where the free throw line is, three point line, and out of bounce is. Also they have four black, blue, and orange goals. the basketball courts are surounded with trees of all sort like pine, dogwood, and so on. The black top is very hard that when you fall you say, Wow, that hurt." It also leaves strawberrys and bruises on your knees.

As you turn to your left you will see a concrete stairway that has a black metel bar that you hold on to. It leads up to a gray wooden building that has two bathrooms and changing rooms. One for the girls that is on the right and one for the boys that's on the left. You will keep walking in and you will see a desk to your left that says, "Sign up and pay to swim." the desk has lockers behind it that have names of the lifeguards. As you walk about four feet from the desk you will see a blue sparkling pool that when you look at it, it makes your eyes water and invites you to dive in. It is three feet to fourteen feet deep. On the sides of the pool are two five feet lifeguard stands. They are wooden and painted red. Their are also two white divenboards, one tall and one short.

As you look to the right of the pool you'll see a playground area with two merry-go-rounds that are purple and blue that six people can ride. You will also see eight metel swings that when you swing on them you feel like you are going to fly off like a bird. there is also a gray wooden building that has six or seven picnic tables so that people can come and have lunch in the sun. The picnic tables are white and gray. They are also 5 ft by 3 ft long. The building is open on all four sides. It is a square shaped building. To the left of the building is a metel stick sticking up out of the ground, and about 7 ft away from it is another metel stick, and it is a game called horseshoes.

Now you can see why I picked this place to describe for you. Don't you think this is a great place to describe? Wouldn't you like to visit it so that you can see it for yourself?

Sample Set #1
Descriptive — "A Place to Have Fun"

Example #10

The place where I go to have fun is Carowinds. It has lots of games, music, food, and clothing. Also the rides are awsome too.

My first reason is that it has lots of games like throw a baseball and knock the pins down and you win a stuffed animal. there lots of clothing shops like the tweety shop it's cool it has lots of tweety's. The music is old fashion but ok it's not really bad. The food there is great it has seafood, old fashion food, and fast food.

My second reason is the rides there awsome. The vortex is sort of uncomfortable the seats are bicylce seats. It starts off slow and then go's really fast and go's upside down. The hurrier is ok it starts off really fast it makes lots of people sick. White water was really cool it go's up slow then flys down and get's people all wet. Plus the swinging ship was cool but it started raining and it wouldn't stop until about an hour later.

My conclusion is that it has lots of games, food, music, and clothing. Also it has awesome rides.

Sample Set #1
Descriptive — "A Place to Have Fun"

Example #11

Tell me! What do you think about when writing about a place where people have fun? I think of Malls. Hanging out with your friends, shopping for new kix/shoes, and the good food, which I will elaborate more on in the following lines, but not exactly in that order.

Hanging out not alone, of course, but with five of your friends in the mall is fun. The great big walls that are full of marble and cement and the smell of marble in the air keeps me coming back. The mall is like a enormously big grocery store. It's got all of your needs just with high and low prices. The mall floor is a purple and green design, white purple green. It smells like buble gum chewed and thrown away but still with it's flavory smell. Then when your hanging out and you start getting closer to the stores you was looking for, everything starts turning the color of that sports store, and there-fore also smelling as if your already in the store and all of you are looking at the same thing, the Nike air max. The black and white shoe takes your breath away until that hunger starts setten in and you don't smell the store any more or the smelly gym sock smell or the cement marble and buble gum rolled into one, but the food cort which I will elaborate on more in the coming paragraph.

The food cort smells like Chinese food, Mc Donalds chicken nuggets and Sabarrow Pizza rolled into one. While your smelling all this you are getting hungrier than a full grown mama bear out of hibernation. Just then you and your friends decide your eating at Sabarrow Pizza. As your walking over the smell of pizza gets stronger like a person throughing up in one part of the room and then the other while all other smells seem just too be clocked out. While the look of the mall starts looking like a restaurant with red and white floor tile, pizza menus all on the wall and behind the glass on the counter where the pizza is made. We tell the lady what we want. She slides over on a plate to the cashier. She gives us a drink, and amount of money it is. Then were off to eat where ever we want. After we finish eating someone says, "I'm going to get a shirt." So we finish quick and set off for the Gap. Which I will say more about in the next paragraph.

The Gap smelled just like the food cort since it was right across from it. My friend was looking at the Ginco shirts and found a black one that said, "Not here not there but everywhere." The store was playing music from some unknown place. The walks were painted fushea and blue which looked cool.

That's a place I think of when you think of somewhere people go to have fun, to hang out, shop, and eat good food. It just makes me feel good. Where do you hangout at? But that's another story.

Scores and Analyses for Sample Set #1

Descriptive — "Fun Place"

Descriptive ("Fun Place") — Example #1

Since spelling and mechanics errors are scored separately in North Carolina, this paper earned a rather **high** score of a **3.5**. It began with an onomatopoeia and contained three clear, fairly well developed focal points (the beach sounds, the sand, and the ocean floor). It maintained a fairly clear visual picture throughout most of the essay slipping only a few times. There is some detail like "little birds, snails and pincher's" and " jagged shells and rocks," but more could be used for a higher score. Vocabulary (though misspelled) was more than adequate. This paper probably did not score higher due to the occasional slip from visual to other senses that did not enhance what you could see ("the sand feels cold from the ocean water" and "the ocean tastes like..."), the need for more nitty-gritty details, and the lack of a lot of strong, action verbs.

Descriptive ("Fun Place") — Example #2

This is a good, solid **medium** paper. It received a **3**. It is organized with three focal points, the slide, the merry-go-round, and the jungle gym, but it lacks the nitty-gritty detail necessary for a higher score. It begins with a grabber, but the introduction is not fully developed. The writer also gets off the topic and inserts himself/herself into the paper ("I love Ol' Rusty. I just wouldn't suggest any one with a weak stomach......"). Vocabulary is lack-luster, and while you can visualize the Jungle Gym, some of the other descriptions are not clear.

Descriptive ("Fun Place") — Example #3

Although this paper begins with a question, attempts good vocabulary ("pulcurtudinous"), and has three clear focal points (the pool, the snack bar, and an ice cream truck), it lacks detail necessary for the reader to picture the place clearly. It is a **low medium** and received a score of **2.5**. The lower score is also probably because the writer got off the topic and turned the essay into a narrative. There are few action verbs, the conclusion is also poorly developed, and the lack of transitions takes away from the clarity.

Descriptive ("Fun Place") — Example #4

This paper is a typical **medium** and received a **3** from the official scorers. It is organized, begins with an onomatopoeia, uses a few good vocabulary words ("crimson," "azure," "chilling"), and contains three clear focal points — the lake, the woods, and the gym. Transitions are cleverly used ("Out of the woods and across from the lake there is a gym."), but more strong, active verbs are needed. While the author paints a fairly clear picture of the park, the lack of nitty-gritty details probably kept it from receiving a higher score. For example, the writer talked about machines for building strength but went no further in describing them.

Descriptive ("Fun Place") — Example #5

This **below average**, low paper begins well, but fails to develop the topic and, at times, turns into an expository/clarification essay ("My first reason..."). It received a **2** on the test probably because it did not stick to the descriptive style of writing and because it lacks three focal points for one place. Instead, it talks about three places where the writer has experienced fun. The paper also lacks support and good vocabulary as well. What probably kept this paper from receiving a lower score are the small descriptions within the three middle paragraphs. Obviously, following the directions of a descriptive essay would raise this paper's score.

Descriptive ("Fun Place") — Example #6

There is no question that this is a **high** paper. It received the top score of a **4**. It is well organized and developed. The three focal points — the sounds, the fun things to do, the scenery — are well supported with nitty-gritty detail

("To begin with you notice all of the trees..... There are dogwoods just blossoming and little maple trees that have been freshly planted. Tall oak trees provide shade....."). Vocabulary is excellent ("exhilarating," "engulfed," "refreshing"), and literary devices abound (onomatopoeia, similes, alliteration). The author frequently uses strong verbs as well.

Descriptive ("Fun Place") — Example #7

This paper received a **1.5** and is clearly a **low** essay. The only thing that saved this paper from receiving a **1** or lower was the skimpy attempt at a description of the ancient creatures and the octopus that could be found in the museum and the obvious attempt at some kind of organization (a beginning, a middle of some sort, and a conclusion). The introduction and conclusion are dull. No interesting vocabulary or strong verbs grace the essay, and the reader cannot picture the museum at all. There are no focal points, transitions, or details to help.

Descriptive ("Fun Place") — Example #8

While this essay is obviously higher than the previous one, it is only a **low medium** essay that received a score of **2.5**. There are three focal points — the rides, the games, and the shows — but they are poorly described with very few details. The description of the rides is the only one the reader can picture. This paragraph probably kept the paper from receiving a lower score. Strong verbs, more details, sticking to the topic (the writer begins to talk about the prizes without describing anything else about the games), and good vocabulary, would raise the score of this paper.

Descriptive ("Fun Place") — Example #9

This paper, obviously, should receive a **high** score, and it did — a **4**. While the introduction and conclusion might be better developed, the rest of the essay is excellent. The three focal points — the pool, the basketball courts, and the playground — are vividly described with nitty-gritty detail, strong verbs, good vocabulary, and great transitions. The writer uses transition devices to walk you through the park which orients you to where you are. Details are so vivid ("blue sparkling pool that when you look at it, it makes your eyes water and invites you to dive in. It is three feet to fourteen feet deep") that you feel as if you are there.

Descriptive ("Fun Place") — Example #10

This paper abandoned the descriptive genre and changed to an expository/clarification essay ("My first reason," "My second reason"). Despite this, however, it scored a **2** on the test. I would rate it a **low**. There are no strong verbs or really good vocabulary. While there are focal points mentioned in the introduction (the games, the music, the food, the clothing, and the rides), only one is developed. The others are mentioned without any detail or description. The description of the one ride, the "vortex" probably kept it from receiving a lower score.

Descriptive ("Fun Place") — Example #11

The three fairly well developed focal points (hanging out, shopping, food), obvious organization with a good introduction and conclusion, and clear picture of the mall itself earned this paper a **high** of a **3.5**. The description flags a little when the writer talks about the good "cort" and gets off the topic, writing about getting the food rather than describing it. This plus a lack of really good vocabulary probably kept this essay from receiving a higher score.

2. Expository/Clarification Examples

TOPIC: "What book would you recommend that the whole class read? Give reasons why you recommend this book."

NOTE: Because scoring differs from state to state, these samples are scored **HIGH**, **MEDIUM**, **LOW**, or **ZERO** for ease of translation.

Sample Set #2
Expository/Clarification — "Book"

Example #1

Book for Class to Read

One book that I suggest the whole class to read is <u>The Diary Of Anne Frank</u>. This book narrates the many hardships that a thirteen year-old girl, Anne, had to endure during the World War II. The story began with Anne and her family hiding in an attic of a spice factory. Anne must spend most of her day in silences, and can not use the bathroom between seven o'clock in the morning till six o'clock at night. The author, Anne, in her writing conveys all the emotions she felt, and the settings are vividly describe. Although the story has a sad end, it is truly moving.

There is three main reasons why I choose this book. The first reason is that the students can easily relate to this book, and it can also teach the students about World War II. The last important reason why this is a good book for the class to read is because it is very moving.

This is a book that the student can relate to because it is about a girl our age. Anne had the same hopes and fears that we now experience. For this reason, the students can easily understand the feelings of the main character. For instance, Anne want to be a writer, and doesn't everyone have a dream?

Through discussion, the students can learn much about the World War II. The students learn first hand about the daily life of Jews. They also learn about Hitler and the Gustapo policemen. The students are also exposed to the concentration camps and much more. So by reading this book, the students can learn some history.

The last reason is that the book is very well written. It is so well written that the reader can feel what the character is feeling. It is almost as if you were Anne! For example, when the author describes a jubilant scene, you feel happy too. The book is also interesting and keep you hooked. Once you pick up the book you can't put it down until you finish it.

I believe the student will truly enjoy this book because of its cultural content. This book not only move the students emotionally, but also is educationally beneficial! All in all, this is a great book for the class to read.

Sample Set #2
Expository/Clarification — "Book"

Example #2

The Book

Yesterday my teacher chose me to pick a book that the class was to read. I told her that "The Incredible Journey" would be a good because of how the animal's pulled together to get to their master.

It will also show the students how to write well and how description can make a story good or bad.

Today she had "The Incredible Journey" and all the kids loved the beginning and my teacher was happy.

Sample Set #2
Expository/Clarification — "Book"

Example #3

A Good Book

The book I would choose I would probaly choose is <u>Jurassic Park</u>. <u>Jurrusic Park</u> is about a scientist who finds a huge mineral stone. When he was polishing it he finds a miscita in it. Since the rock was made millions of years before the mescita it had to be old.

The scientist takes the stone to another scientist were they find out the mosquito was over a million years old. Since the bug was in the ancient rock it had to be an ancient bug. Happened to contain DNA from dinasaurs. From their other scientist were able to reproduce the DNA and create real dinasaurs.

After hearing this a rich dinosaur searcher hired some private scientist and make his own dinosaurs. He soon makes over 250 dinasaurs. He has them all on a island that he will turn into a amusement park. The park was about to open when something went wrong.

The reason I would recomend this book is because it is very intrirty. When I first heard about it I thought it would be horribly. But after I read it I found out I was totally wrong. It was amazing in explain the detail even though it can be a little grousome it is a good book.

Sample Set #2
Expository/Clarification — "Book"

Example #4

The Book to Read to All

My teacher has asked me to write a paper explaining about a favorite book. It is <u>The Once and Future King</u> by J.H. White. This book shows the life of King Arthur to its fullest. In this story there is love, forbidden to those who want it. Also war, death at the hands of the mightest, and the dark secrets that creep between every crack in the wall like cockroaches.

The darkest secrets of this book effect love and war. Dark secrets and stories about people doing what shouldn't be told. For instance, when Guenevere and Lancelot fall in love, King Arthur lets them carry it on. Only if someone else were to reveal it, would he have to pontificate the matter in court.

Another good point about the book is the war involved. When Arthur started the Knights of the Round Table, his table given to him by Guenevere's father, all the knights desired to become part of it. He demanded that they all do good deeds. For only good deeds prevail at death.

Last of all, but already partially mentioned in this tragic tale when Lancelot beseached the Queen's love and she accepted. The funny thing is exactly what happened, one part of the book told them sneaking to each other's room. A good example would be the night when Arthur was away. Lancelot's friendly knight warned him he would be caught. But Lancelot went anyways for love.

Through hardships to the downfall of Arthur, love prevailed. This shows that war can be caused by love, but only good deeds can be caused within oneself. Dark secrets may lead the way to death when they are told, but whatever happens, people at least in this tale, follow their hearts' desire. Fearing the consequences, but still facing them head on.

Sample Set #2
Expository/Clarification — "Book"

Example #5

My english teacher asked me to recomend a book for our class to read. The book I would recommend is <u>A Wrinkle In Time</u> because it is an eighth grade reading level and a book of all kinds, mystery, drama, and all that stuff.

The reason this book is so great is you never know whats going to happen next. For instance Meg, the main character, has to figure out a way to destroy a big brain called It who has her brother under his control.

Another time in the drama part is when Meg finally sees her father again after 10 years.

I think anybody who knows how to read would enjoy this book more than any book in the whole world.

Sample Set #2
Expository/Clarification — "Book"

Example #6

A Book for My Class

I recomend the book <u>A Spell for Chameleon</u> by Piers Anthony. It is a great book to read. It has everything in it to make you want to read it. It has funny jokes, adventure, and magic. It is also good because it keeps you wanting to read it.

<u>A Spell for Chameleon</u> is about finding a special spell for someone. It has puns in it. And that makes it funny. When he goes looking for his spell he meets all kinds of intersting people like centaurs and a magican who lives in a castle. This keeps the book intersting.

This book keeps you wanting to read it. The hero goes hunting for his spell and gets into some scary scraps. There are fight places that also keep you wanting to read. You keep reading because you want to find out what happens.

A Spell for Cameleon is a good book. I recomend it to the class to read. Everyone, even the teacher will like it.

Sample Set #2
Expository/Clarification — "Book"

Example #7

<u>Animal Farm</u>, a Book with a Message

Recommend a book for the class to read? That is no problem! I recently read a book that every eighth grade student should read as soon as they can — <u>Animal Farm</u> by George Orwell. "Why read this book?" you ask. Besides being an intreguing tale of treachery and trickery that keeps even reluctant readers hooked, it is a story within a story that tells about the Russian Revolution in metaphor. George Orwell's book is also a message about the wrongs of totalitarianism. Even though you can read this book in only a few hours, it is one that no reader could ever forget.

In the first place, <u>Animal Farm</u> is the kind of book that appeals to eighth graders (after all, I am an eighth grader, and I loved it) because the action never stops. There is trickery as Napoleon manages to change the basic rules of the new farm and treachery as he gets rid of Snowball. The twists and turns of the plot twine around the reader's mind like a cudzu (sp. ?) vine, tugging and pulling the reader further and further into the plot and not letting go until the very end when the pigs are really humans in pork skin. This is a book you can't put down.

<u>Animal Farm</u> also grips the reader because of its hidden metaphor. It isn't really a book about pigs and farm animals. It tells the story of the Russian Revolution with the animals representing real people, like Napoleon being Stalin and Snowball being Trotsky. What a great way to study history painlessly! We eighth graders love hidden meanings and hunting for things. This book really lets us hunt and think and compare ideas about how bad totalitarianism is. Orwell even says in the introduction that his book is a protest against "all the horrors of totalitarianism." It's fun to learn things in this manner.

Finally, I recommend the book <u>Animal Farm</u> to be read by the class because it is one of those books that you read, like <u>Charlotte's Web</u> and Dr. Seuss's <u>Green Eggs and Ham</u> that you never ever forget. When my dad recommended this book to me, he told me that he had read it twenty years ago and he still remembered it today. Perhaps it is the fact that the story is a metaphor for a historical event or perhaps it is the unforgettable characters like Molly, Snowball, Napoleon, and the bleating sheep that make this book so unforgettable. In any case, this is one book that <u>this</u> eighth grader will not forget very soon.

In conclusion, I heartily recommend the book <u>Animal Farm</u> to be read by the class. It is a classic story that not only keeps the reader hooked, but it also has hidden meanings to hunt for. It is a book that my fellow eighth graders will not forget. Like the memory of a great football game where everything goes right, the book <u>Animal Farm</u> stays in your mind for a long time.

Scores and Analyses for Sample Set #2

Expository/Clarification — "Book"

Expository/Clarification ("Book") — Example #1

Despite its difficulties with verbs, this paper would score **high**. There are not enough transitions, but the organization is obvious. The vocabulary ("relate," "jubilant") is excellent. Sentence structure varies. There are some mechanical difficulties, but the overall essay sticks to the topic and explains the topic well with three distinct reasons why the author recommends this book. The introduction and conclusion also are well done except that the student, for greater clarity, could have restated the three reasons why he/she recommended the book.

Expository/Clarification ("Book") — Example #2

While this is obviously a **low** scoring paper, it would not receive the lowest score. On the test, the actual score probably would depend on the readers. The student does stick to the topic and does give two reasons for his/her choice of book. There is also some evidence of organization (note the three paragraphs) Aside from the other errors, there is no support for the topic, and this is what cinches the low score. With some support, vocabulary, and a conclusion, this could easily have scored in the medium range.

Expository/Clarification ("Book") — Example #3

While, at first glance, this looks like a well-organized essay, it is not. While it does have a rudimentary introduction, the rest follows no pattern, and there is no conclusion. In addition, it wanders off the topic. The topic was to recommend a book and give the reasons why you recommend the book. This essay, however, is a synopsis of the plot of a book. For this reason, this paper would score a **low**. Not until the last paragraph does the student give any reasons why anyone should read the book. It is this paragraph which raises the score from **unscorable** to a **1**. There are also numerous mechanical errors. I think the writer has abandoned the use of commas! An attempt was made to include a good vocabulary ("reproduce"), but one of the words he/she tried to use, "intrirty," is so misspelled that the reader cannot discern its origin.

Expository/Clarification ("Book") — Example #4

This paper typifies what I call the "Gifted Hole" that bright children fall into when they write essays. Despite the misuse of "pontificate," the vocabulary is excellent ("breached," "prevail," "tragic," etc.), and the student even includes an appropriately used simile. Sentence structure is varied, and the piece is basically well-written. It is not, however, on the topic at all. This paper would be **unscorable** because, no matter how well written it may be, it does not address the topic. It tells the tale of the book and discusses it instead of giving reasons why it should be read.

This is the hardest kind of paper to score because the teacher in us wants to score it higher because of the writing. We cannot succumb! The scorers of the actual test are ruthless in this respect. Papers **must** stick to the topic. This student even announces in the first sentence that he/she is writing a paper "explaining about a favorite book" rather than putting forth reasons why a teacher should require the entire class to read the book.

Expository/Clarification ("Book") — Example #5

This paper, despite its brevity, would score in the **medium** range. Vocabulary and sentence structure are adequate. There is some obvious organization in an introduction, a middle that gives examples, and a brief conclusion. The student would not earn a higher grade because of the paucity of support. He/she really only gives two reasons and supplies support for only one of them.

Expository/Clarification ("Book") — Example #6

This is a good, solid **medium** paper. On the actual test, it would most certainly score a **4** on a 1-6 scale. It is organized with a beginning, a middle, and an end, and it has support, but the introduction and conclusion are not fully developed. There are no transitions. Vocabulary use is good but nothing out of the ordinary. Support is there, but it is not enough to earn the paper a higher grade. Sentence structure is mostly simple. And, while there are not too many mechanical errors, it is not a paper that stands out as did Example #1.

Expository/Clarification ("Book") — Example #7

There is no question about the score for this paper. It is a **high**. In fact, because it is so well focused on the topic, so well organized, and uses sophisticated vocabulary ("intriguing," "treachery"), varied sentence structure, similes ("like a cudzo vine"), humor, flair, and even a quote from Orwell, that it would probably receive the top score on the writing assessment test. This student shows knowledge of the book and history, revealing an insight beyond his/her years. (We studied the book in class, but the scorers do not know that, nor is that fact relevant to the essay.)

3. More Expository/Clarification Examples

TOPIC: "If your principal asked you to head a committee to improve the lunchroom conditions, what would you suggest?"

NOTE: Because scoring differs from state to state, these samples are scored **HIGH**, **MEDIUM**, **LOW**, or **ZERO** for ease of translation.

Sample Set #3
Expository/Clarification — "Lunchroom"

Example #1

Changing the Cafeteria

If the principal appointed me to committee the lunchroom I would higher an exterminator to get rid of all the rats and roaches. Let the kids have a day when they get pizza delivered. Then I would higher new cooks to cook the food. The food would have to taste and look good.

If I did this the students would want to come to the lunchroom and would not talk about if parents would send their kids here just for the lunchroom.

If the kids are good I will make the servers be happy when they serve, and I will get 102 Jamz D.J. and put him on the stage so the students will be able to dance but only on the stage and if they be bad I will remove the D.J. and take away their pizza day.

If I did all this the lunchroom will be known nationwide and the kids will want to come even more.

The people with their own lunches will have to sit in one area and the people who eat the lunchroom sit anywhere except with the people with their own lunches. That would help the school out because people would want to buy lunches and it will bring more money.

The End

Sample Set #3
Expository/Clarification — "Lunchroom"

Example #2

Lunch at Westwood

Students aren't enjoying lunch time. There seems to be something wrong with the way they're handling it. I think I have some good ideas for a good way of change.

First, people come in, and try to pry themselves into the lunch line. On certain days you might have to wait in line for 20 minutes. By the time you sit down to eat, you only have about five minutes to eat. If we expand the time to 45 minutes — as much as a regular period — people will be much more pleased.

Second, people want to sit by their friends. The regulations we have now prevent us from sitting with anyone but whom is in your FAME class. There could be a sheet where you sign up to sit at certain tables for the whole year. That way there won't be as much "table-hopping." A happy student is a good student.

Another problem is the temperature. On some days, when it's cold outside, the Cafeteria may be down to 60. It is very uncomfortable. If the Cafeteria was set at a temperature that was comfortable, considering the outside climate, we could improve comfortness.

Another idea could be to paint the awfully dull walls blue. It has been proven that blue slows down the activity rate in your body. It would be hard to do, but maybe on a long holiday or even over the summer, it could be accomplished.

I hope you take some of my ideas to the fullest. I think this could be a good way to an enjoyable, instead of horrid, lunch period. From now on Westwood could have the best lunch time ever.

Sample Set #3
Expository/Clarification — "Lunchroom"

Example #3

Lunchroom Improvements. We Need 'Em

When I envision our school cafeteria, images of wretched food and unbelievable noise come to mind. It is an awful place, a place most students want to avoid. There is room for much improvement!

If I were to be appointed to a committee to improve the lunchroom, the first thing I would do would be to take some kind of input from the actual consumers, the students. I would find out what kind of foods the majority of people would prefer. This menu wouldn't be all pepperoni pizza and coke, as some of you probably visioned. It would be a balanced, nutritious meal, complete with all four of the food groups.

As I complete my first changes, I would then deal with the Food Service Workers, better known as Cafeterians. I personally have no problem with them, yet my peers insist that they are rude, unsanitary, and cranky. Maybe a routine check of the sanitation devices, i.e. dishwashers, ovens, freezers, so on and so forth, would help.

From what I witness, most Cafeterians don't use plastic rubber gloves while handling unprepared food. This discusts me to no avail. I can not eat in a cafeteria knowing that the food I am about to digest has been handled by a pair of dirty, greasy, grimy hands.

More supervision is needed in our cafeteria. As I mentioned earlier, the decibel level in our lunchroom reaches unbearable heights. Granted, the noise is generated from talking, but if you've ever been in an enclosed room with three-hundred "talking" eighth graders, I need to explain no longer.

I feel that if there was more supervision, the pupils wouldn't be inclined to speak as loudly as they regularly would; which takes me directly into my next subject — punishment.

Punishment should be doled out upon serious infractions of THE RULES. The rules include not throwing food, no yelling, no fighting, and no breaking manditory school rules. Infractions of the policy will result in eating lunch on stage, in plain view of the entire student body, next to the principal of the school. Self-ridicule and just plain embarrassment will make this a dreaded punishment never voluntarily experienced again.

In conclusion, I feel that the lunchroom in our school is adequate, if not average, with a few glaring deficienceys. And, that's why I'm here.

Sample Set #3
Expository/Clarification — "Lunchroom"

Example #4

The New Lunchroom

The lunchroom was old. First the bricks lost their color of white. Second the tables bent in different directions. Third the food tasted hard and crusty. Fourth the floor was scattered with litter and food.

One day, the principal called me up and asked me to be the leader of the comitee to improve the lunchroom.

The first day we decided we would repaint the whole building. We sent the children outside to eat, and then we started painting. First we jet-sprayed the walls with water to get the extra paint off the walls. After that we power-sprayed the walls white. Third we took rollers and painted the places where we missed.

The second day we decided to switch the chairs and tables that were destroyed. First we moved the chairs and tables out, so they could be recycled. Second we went out and bought new chairs and tables that felt more comfortable. Third we moved them into different places, so the lunchroom would look a lot neater and better.

The third day we put trashcans by the tables, so people could throw away their trash. Second we called fast food restaurants to sell food at our lunchroom. Third we threw away the hard and crusty food (that tasted like astro turf) into the trashcan. Fourth, we got a new order of food that tasted a lot better, and a lot better looking.

On the fourth day we started to plant flowers around the lunchroom, so it would look nice and clean.

On the fifth day we decided to put a radio in. First we hooked up speakers around the lunchroom. After that we hooked up all the wires and see how the lunchroom would take it. The school shook like an earthquake.

When the lunchroom reopened, everyone went in to see what it would look like. It looked so nice that the principal awarded us with a trophy and some money. After the cleanup, no one ever trashed the lunchroom again.

Sample Set #3
Expository/Clarification — "Lunchroom"

Example #5

"Improve The Lunchroom!"

"Improve the Lunchroom!" our principal demanded. He said if the lunchroom wasn't fixed up in less than two weeks he would shut it down. "I'm tired of all the complaints I'm getting." he said.

We got down to buiseness right away. First we thought the kids should get to vote on what the school serves for each day. Then we thought up some stricter rules to keep everyone under controll. Third we tried to make up privaliges and fun games we could all play to award the students for good behavior. We are even trying to make lunch an hour instead of thirty minutes everyday.

Sample Set #3
Expository/Clarification — "Lunchroom"

Example #6

Lunchroom Improvements

The problem with the lunchroom today one is that it's not very clean. For instance right after the seventh grade eat the eighth grade comes in after them. Crumbs and spilt drinks that seventh graders left, fill the ground along with the tables and seats. I definitely would make sure that the janitors cleaned up the place after each grade ate. Second of all, the cafeteria smells as if a thousand animals were slaughtered there and eggs were cracked then left to rought. Finally, the lunchroom has no personality of it's own, and absolutely nothing to cheer it up a bit. It's just so plan!

The smell that's in the lunchroom I would put an end to by getting rid of any old food that might be left. Then after that was completed I would have people sterilize the lunchroom every week. After that I would put in little airfresheners all over the room not enough to keck (gag) people, just enough to send a slight scent through the air. To make the lunchroom look a little bit better I'd add pictures and decorate the stage with more life, maybe put up some curtains nice curtains and keep them closed all the time.

My ideas would certainly brighten up the cafeteria, and give a little originality to our school's name.

Sample Set #3
Expository/Clarification — "Lunchroom"

Example #7

Lunchroom Food

Lunchroom food is horrible! Have you ever tasted the mystery meat hamburgers there? The chicken is so tough that you think it will turn to shoe leather in your mouth. And those casseroles!!! You could study them for hours and not discover what lurks in them for some poor student to eat. I recommend bringing your own lunch, packed by your loving mother with non-mysterious ingredients.

I usually bring my own lunch, being wise to the horribleness of cafeteria food, but one day last week, I was in a rush and left my lunch bag on the kitchen counter. After a quick look at the lunchroom menu, I decided to go without eating. A "kind" teacher, however, could not stand seeing a poor student go hungry and gave me money to buy a lunch. Naturally, being the considerate kid that I am, I had to get in line behind the other poor unfortunate eighth graders and get a lunch.

With the teacher looking down at me as I sat down at the lunch table with the cafeteria lunch in front of me, I had to eat it. My stomach growled in sympathy with my mouth. Somehow I had to eat that glop. It was a casserole of some sort, buried in a reddish sause and swimming in grease. Green specks of something that was once alive was in there. It looked repulsive. I smiled at the teacher and took a small bite.

It tasted worse than it looked! The grease rolled around on my tongue making the green stuff slide down my throat before I even swallowed. It reminded me of the time I ate dogfood — yuck! I wanted to rolf.

I resolved then and there, as I forced the rest of the mess into my unhappy stomach while smiling at the teacher, that I would never, ever leave my lunch at home again. I had learned my lesson!

Scores and Analyses for Sample Set #3

Expository/Clarification — "Lunchroom"

Expository/Clarification ("Lunchroom") — Example #1

This is a perfect **medium** paper. On the actual test, it would probably receive a score at the high end of the medium range. While it has some serious mechanical errors such as a pointed lack of commas and repeated spelling problems, it is somewhat organized with a beginning and a middle. It lacks a conclusion which alone would prevent this essay from receiving a higher score. There are some specific suggestions that are somewhat developed. The vocabulary is adequate.

Expository/Clarification ("Lunchroom") — Example #2

This paper is obviously a **high**. On the actual test, it might score at the low end of high. The organization is excellent, even to the use of transitions. Vocabulary is also good ("considering," "accomplished," "dull," "expand," etc.) but not outstanding. There are very few errors, and sentence structure is varied. The introduction and conclusion could be better developed, and the three ideas could be stated in each. This is a very good paper with well-developed support and details.

Expository/Clarification ("Lunchroom") — Example #3

Like Example #2, this paper obviously deserves a **high** score. In fact on the actual test, it probably would receive one of the rare top scores granted! It has humor, excellent vocabulary ("mandatory," "peers," "consumers," "granted," "envision," etc.), sophisticated sentence structure, and apart from a few minor spelling errors, few mechanical errors. The organization is also excellent, though the introduction could be a bit better developed to disclose the three suggestions. Support is superior with many details provided. The humor certainly adds to the score. This is definitely a superior essay.

Expository/Clarification ("Lunchroom") — Example #4

This is a tricky one to score. It looks good at first glance, but the student really got off the topic by telling what he/she did to the lunchroom rather than give suggestions as head of a committee. This immediately takes the score down by a few points. The introduction is clever, but the conclusion is weak and gets slightly off topic, telling how happy the students were with the improvements. The overuse of transitions is confusing. There are frequent minor mechanical errors. Vocabulary, while adequate, is nothing to write home about. The student has used two similes which helps, but the fact that the essay gets off the basic topic cannot be ignored. This essay probably would receive a **medium** score because it does not present suggestions, as the prompt demands, but instead states the changes as if they have already been made, and describes their effects.

Expository/Clarification ("Lunchroom") — Example #5

This essay would score a **low** (probably a $^1/_2$ to **1** on the actual test) since it is essentially a list with no support or detail and no conclusion. Vocabulary is adequate, but an essay that is a list with no support cannot score higher than a low since support and focus are the two main things the scorers are looking for in the essays. This essay even strays from the topic in that the student has made a narrative essay out of an expository topic. There is an introduction; the list follows. These keep the essay from being **unscorable**.

Expository/Clarification ("Lunchroom") — Example #6

This essay is a **low medium**. It has a short introduction and conclusion and has support for fixing the smell but only one sentence of support for cheer(ing) it up. There are English and spelling errors (misuse of "it's," for example). Vocabulary is good with use of words such as "slaughtered," "sterilize," and "keck." (The student got this last word from a *Caught'ya* and was told not to use it on the state assessment test as it is an archaic word, but at least he/she tried to use good vocabulary and similes.) Organization and support are the main downfalls of this essay.

Expository/Clarification ("Lunchroom") — Example #7

This paper, like #4 in Set #2 is **unscorable**. It is the hardest type of paper to score since it is well written and coherent (and funny), but if the student does not address the topic, the paper cannot be scored. This example mentions food but has no suggestions to improve the lunchroom. Obviously the student is bright and writes well with a good command of vocabulary, but he/she committed the cardinal sin of not addressing the topic at hand: improvements to the lunchroom. I call this the "gifted hole" into which bright students sometimes tumble. Indeed, one wonders what went through this student's mind as he/she read the topic. Sometimes very bright students dislike the topic so much that they simply refuse to write about it, writing instead about something that pleases them. This writer chose to write a personal narrative. Obviously, he/she had a "beef" with the cafeteria food and wanted to write about it. No matter how well written this paper is, it cannot receive a score on the writing assessment test.

4. Narrative Examples

TOPIC: "Every day you pass a door. It is always locked. One day, as you pass, you notice that the door is open. You step inside. Write a story about what was on the other side of the door."

NOTE: Because scoring differs from state to state, these samples are scored **HIGH**, **MEDIUM**, **LOW**, or **ZERO** for ease of translation.

Sample Set #4
Narrative — "Door"

Example #1

When I go to the garage to get my bike out or skates, I see a door. I always wonder what's inside, but for some mysterios reason it is always locked. One day when I went to get my bike I wanted to open the door and it opened. I was so impressed.

I then decided to check out what was in there. When I went in there I saw a bunch of spider webs on the ceiling. I didn't get to scared. After I passed the spider webs, I saw this beautiful garden. It was full of flowers like daisies.

I soon started to get tired, so I got out of the door. The next day I came and tried to open the door but it just would not open. I soon realized that it was my first and only chance to go in there. After that I never forgot about the garden.

Sample Set #4
Narrative — "Door"

Example #2

You go lock it. And go up staris. And come Back down. It is unlocked and open. Something is say get out the house. Get out the house NOW. You get out of the house. And go to a nobar house that you and your mom know. Call the poilce as soon as you get there. When you get on the Phone be com and make sure you tell every thing. And don't forget to tell your adsdres and Phone number to. When you see your mom or the poilce go outside and meet them.

Sample Set #4
Narrative — "Door"

Example #3

Every day I go past a certain door and every day it is locked. One day I walk past it and it is unlocked. I wondered what was inside so I decided to go in.

The very next day I went in. I opened the door as silently as I could. Then, out came a huge, "Creak!"

"Oh — no!!! Whoever lives here will catch me now," I thought as I ducked behind the bushes. No one came out. I ran inside extremely fast huffing and puffing. You won't believe what happened next!

It was black, pitch plack. Then again I thought I could see large white blanket looking things above and around me. They swirled like ghosts in all directions. I tried to ignore them by walking into the next room. The swirling blankets wouldn't go away. To my horror a high pitched scream rang out of my throat.

The blankets swirled around me faster, faster. I wanted to run away from them but my feet wouldn't move.

"Honey are you okay?" my mother said in her soft, sweet voice that seemed to come from far away.

"Yes," I said that I just had a bad dream. "Yes," I said to myself this time and opened my eyes. "It was all a bad dream."

Sample Set #4
Narrative — "Door"

Example #4

I walk home from school pass a door that is always locked. One day after school while I was walking home the door was unlocked. Then, I slowly walked inside. Soon, I found a staircase next to it was a night in shining armour. Slowly something extraordanary happend. The night in shining armour became a six leged ten armed alien.

I turned away and ran up the crooked stairs, then, I triped. The one eyed six leged ten armed two body alien creature walked closer. I got up and ran to the window. The alien started shooting acid at me. Then, I jumped out the window. The alien turned to stone and I went home. What a day!

Sample Set #4
Narrative — "Door"

Example #5

When I had walk past the door and I had went back. I had open the door I was so scarred. I had look up. I was going around and around. It had feel like some one was turnig me around in a circle.

I saw this big fat thing in there on the cles. When I had look it was on the ground I had saw a sperier. Then the door had close. I was so scared. I did not no want to do when that door had clesed. I saw some cloes the had some back salf on it. I was looking at the balck caest. It got hot and hot in the clocet.

the end

Sample Set #4
Narrative — "Door"

Example #6

   I walk to and from school every day exsept Saturday and senday of corse. I always pass a locked door but this time it is unlocked and I take a step closer and it open quit quickly. There is a glary light inside the creepy door. Inside the glary light there is a creepy I mean creepy figure. It looked lopsided. I was so puzzled?

   I took a few more steps and ...SMACK...the door shut loder than an atomike bomb. Well, maybe not quit that loud. Then...B-O-O-O..., my own family every one scared me half to death. I was so terrifed.

Sample Set #4
Narrative — "Door"

Example #7

Every day on my way home from school, I walk past a door that is always locked. Today, it was opened. I decided to voyage inside and explore. I cautiously entered the open door and stepped inside. Then, I found out that there was no floor under me.

"AAAAHHHHHHHHH!.," I shrieked as loud as a siren. The sound echoed off the walls of what seemed to be an endless pit as I fell and tumbled down and down. However, I soon found out it was not endless as soon as I hit the ground with an extremely loud thud.

I found that I was on the ground surrounded by snakes. They all glared at me with eerie, beady red eyes, ready to strike if I moved a muscle. Horrified, I held myself more stiff than petrified wood. I then did the only thing I could do.

"HELP!" I yelled at the top of my lungs. My heart pounded as loud as thunder. Maybe even louder as it seemed to echo off the walls of the pit. The snakes slithered closer to me, their winding bodies looking like dark spaghetti twisted together and moving. Then, from somewhere in the dark, a door opened with a creak, shining a light on the snakes and me. I lept up and rushed through the door as fast as possible, trying to leap over the snakes in my best ballet jump.

"I need to get home," I said.

"I know how to get you home," said a little green man who had suddenly appeared on the other side of the door. "We can throw a rope ladder up to attatch it to the doorknob way up there. But, we will have an extraordinary chance of being eaten by snakes on the way. They are still on the other side of this door." "Anything is what I will do to get home," I said confidently. "We can do it."

So the little green man and I cauciously opened the door to the room with the snakes. We streaked through the room to the side where the doorknob was way above us. It seemed billions of miles away. I just stared up at the doorknob above us, wondering if it was possible for me to get home. The little green man took a rope from around his waste and threw it up high, so high it disappeared.

Then I saw the rope ladder was attached to the doorknob. I jumped for joy onto the bottom of the ladder. I climbed as fast as I could, higher and higher. I felt I climbed up miles. Then before I knew it, I was out of the pit and through the door to outside.

"Thanks," I called down to the little green man who was staring up at me from the bottom of the rope ladder and waving goodbye.

I think that was a very scary time. I hope I never get that scared again. I know I will never go through opened doors ever again without knowing what is on the other side.

Sample Set #4
Narrative — "Door"

Example #8

Every day, you walk past a door certain door and it always locked. One day however, you walk by and notice it is unlocked. When you pasted a door the door is unlocked and you go in the door to see what's in there. The room is dark and scary. You cut on the light to see in the room the room is imtea. The room had nothing in it. No bad no dresot no mirro it had no tv in t. "It was just imtea."

That is my sory.

Sample Set #4
Narrative — "Door"

Example #9

It was a beautifull Saturday morning in Gainesville, Florida. Mom and Dad had gone to a confrence and I got to stay home. I dicided to go into my parents room. I looked up and down and back and forth like a spy. I was eying my parents closet that was always locked like a prison.

I built up the courage to walk over. Without having to touch the knob it opened. I slowly creped inside, and my eyes got used to the blinding light inside the closet. Surprisingly, there were no dirty socks hanging off the shelves. Instead, there were scattered pieces of moss hanging off tiny palm trees. Instead of shirts spraled across the floor there were ponds with huge orange swans. There were even stars in the sky when the sun was shining.

I steped out for a second to make sure I wasn't dreaming when the door closed behind me. I tried franticly to get it opened but it was locked again! Now the door that was locked for years finally beheld it's magic, but now it is locked again forever.

Sample Set #4
Narrative — "Door"

Example #10

Maybe it is a man. A mean man. Maybe it was his secreat hideout. Or maybe is is a kid. A kid that goes at school. Maybe it is the kid workshop. When I went inside and what did I see. I saw a kid. I was right it was a kid. I guess a really good guess it was.

Sample Set #4
Narrative — "Door"

Example #11

One day, after Girl Scouts, I walked past a door that is usually locked. I found the door unlocked. Now this is strange. I decided to go inside. The walls were covered in greenish mold!

I walked farther down the hall. I then came to a room. The room was a bathroom. I peeked in. There was an old-fashioned bathtub in the corner.

I walked in to the bathroom. I found a trap door. Hesitently, I opened it. I found beautiful jewelry. The jewelry was gold, pearl, and silver.

I closed the trap door and went across the hall. I found a bedroom. There was curtains around a bed. I opened the curtains. The bed was dark purple.

I walked down the hall even farther and found a staircase. I went up the staircase and found another hall. I walked down this hall.

Unexpectedly, everything modernized! The walls became black. It was a strange black. Then, paintings appeared on the walls. Paintings of famous singers.

I was stunned! I ran all the way home. When I got home nobody believed my story.

I still can't figure out what happened behind that door!

The End

Sample Set #4
Narrative — "Door"

Example #12

I always walk by an old house that is locked. On a Sat. I found that the door was standing wide open. My mom had always taught me not to go in to other peoples houses. I stopped, and paused. I asked myself if I sould go in or not. Since the house was abanted why not go in and take a peek.

I walked up the stairs and peeked into the old house. All a sudden a bird flew out of the old house. A shiver ran down my spine and I started to shake. I had an urge to go inside so I walked inside and all a sudden the door slamed behind me and the room grew dark.

The next thing I knew the room turned into a magic world. Through a light mist I could see a magical city, lit up by lights that made it look like Cindarella's castle with waterfalls around it. There were beasts, wild animals, monsters who lumbered around on green medows, and a giant doll who started crying when she saw me. The magic world started to flood with the tears of the doll. All of a sudden this giant dargon comes out and trys to burn me but I smiled at him and he asked me, "Do you need a ride?"

I answered, "yes."

The dargon flew me to an edge of a forest. He said, "If you need me again shout "tree."

I walked into the forest. Half way a tree grabed me and then all the trees grabed me. One of the trees made a fire out of its own branches and another made a pot out of bark and put water, spices, and fruits in it. As far as I could see they wanted to make a stew out of me! Then I rembered to yell, "tree." I shouted "TREE" at the top of my lungs and then the dargon appared out of nowhere roaring at the top of his lungs, and spiting out fire.

The fire burned the trees but it didn't burn me for some reason. I thougt it was the weirdest thing so I asked the firendly dargon and he told me that since I'm not a thing that lives here, in the old house, I can't get hurt.

I asked him how to get out of the old house and he said he would take me but it might take us a while and there were a lot of demons like the trees who made stew that would want to try to hurt me. After a while we came upon a ghost that looked like it was mist inside white sheets. The dargon knew how to get rid of him. All he had to do was sing a song but he didn't know any songs to sing so I started to sing "You Are My Sun Shine." The ghost started to disapare and we were on are way agian.

The next stop was to the exit. I fell asleep after a while right on the dargons back. When I woke up I was on the grass in my own back yard. I ran up to the door and my mom was waiting for me. She wasn't worried. I hadn't been gone very long. Maybe she knew about dargons and little girls...

Sample Set #4
Narrative — "Door"

Example #13

I always walk by this door the door is always locked, but one day it was open so I decided to go in. You will never ges what I found.

I went down a very dark tunel. It smelled like something died in here, finaly I got to the end of the tunel. And I found an old amusement park! I decided to take a look around it was etarordnary I had never seen anything like it.

While I was walking around I found a very big swich. I tried to pull it but it was hard so I pulled it down the power came on. I went to look for the the games but ensted I found the rides. Neat! This ride looked famtastick, it was called the swirley so I got in it made me extreamly disey I almost threw up but I held it in.

Then I found the video games! They had some very old games this one was put out of the market for being to vilent I found a quarter so I played a game that was my day.

That was a very fun and exsited so I liked It very much that was a fun day. And very nice day.

Sample Set #4
Narrative — "Door"

Example #14

One day after school my friend and I past a house. The house was big and black and white. When we past the house we notice that the door was open. Then we looked inside. The house was emty. Then we looked more.

First, we looked for foot prints. There where mud prints all on the carpet leding to all the rooms. Then we panitce. "There mustd have been robbed," said my friend. "Yes they musted haved been robbed," repild Sally. "I think we sould call my mom," said Sally.

Next, we called my mom but all she said was, "Quite goffing off." Then she said, "I got to go back to working. Then we called my dad. All he said is that "my mind was playing trick on me." I tryed to ixspain that they where robbed. All he said is, "go do your home work drauger.

Last we called Mrs. Stallbom. She said they where not robbed. That they where moving. I was so that they where not robbed but sad that they were moving. Now I was really sad thay my best friend was moving.

Scores and Analyses for Sample Set #4

Narrative — "Door"

Narrative — Example #1

This example has a definite beginning, middle, and end, wrapping up the story quite nicely. It stays on the topic and even has some description in the middle paragraph (the garden). Mechanics are pretty good, and vocabulary is adequate. I score this paper a **medium** because it lacks detail in the middle, has no attempt at a conversation, and the story needs to be expanded. It is an average paper with nothing special about it.

Narrative — Example #2

This example would have to be **unscorable**. First of all, it never addresses the topic of writing a story about what was on the other side of the door. In fact it never mentions the word "door." It also immediately turns into a how to, expository paper for a child who finds trouble: "Call the poilce as soon as you get there. When you get on the Phone be com and make sure you tell everything." There is no dialogue or good vocabulary.

Narrative — Example #3

This example, although fairly short, is clearly a **high** paper. It has a solid beginning in a paragraph all to itself. The middle is developed with descriptions ("large white blanket looking things"), similes ("like ghosts"), good vocabulary ("ignore," "swirled"), strong verbs ("swirled around me"), and varied sentence structure. The end has a dialogue that is, for the most part, correctly punctuated, and it wraps up the story. This paper would not receive the top score. More detail and more story development would raise the score.

Narrative — Example #4

This paper is a good example of a **low-medium** score. It does have a beginning, a middle, and an end and tells a story. Vocabulary is adequate ("extraordanary"). There is some description of the alien, but the story needs development and detail.

Narrative — Example #5

This example has too many words that are indecipherable ("sperier" and "caest" for example) and, although some sort of story is evident, and there is a semblance of chronological order, there isn't enough to score higher than a **low** (probably a **1**). This is one of the few instances where the spelling is so poor that it interferes with comprehension (and therefore the score).

Narrative — Example #6

This paper has a definite beginning, middle, and end. There is even some descriptive detail in the middle ("creepy figure" "It looked lopsided"), but it is not enough to earn this paper a medium score. Chronological order is not really clear, organization is weak, and the ending doesn't wrap up the story. There is one good vocabulary word ("lopsided"). This would receive a **low** score, but not the lowest.

Narrative — Example #7

This paper is obviously a **high**. In fact it would stand a good chance of receiving the highest score on the writing assessment test. The beginning is well set out, clearly setting the scene. The middle is developed in clear chronological order with descriptions (of the snakes), similes ("as loud as thunder," "more stiff than petrified wood"), dialogue, and detail. There are not too many mechanical errors. Good vocabulary ("extremely," "beady") and strong verbs ("my heart pounded") abound. The story progresses slowly from scene to scene without jumping in action. The end wraps it up with a promise to himself/herself. This is an excellent story with verve, tension, and flair.

Narrative — Example #8

While spelling is obviously a problem ("imtea"), it would not interfere with the score as the words are decipherable. The writer does have a brief beginning and has a little bit of detail in the middle, but there is not really a story here, and organization is poor. This paper would receive a **low** score, probably a **1**.

Narrative — Example #9

This is a good story with a beginning, a fairly well-developed middle, and an end to wrap it up. There are attempts at good vocabulary ("spraled," "scattered"), and even two similes ("like a spy," and "like a prison"). I would give this story a good **medium**. This example would have scored higher with more narrative, a conversation, and a more developed end.

Narrative — Example #10

This paper would be scored a **1** or **unscorable** depending on the reader. It never really addresses the topic or mentions the door. The speculation about the "kid," however, could be interpreted as being on topic enough to give it a **1**. This is not really a narrative, but a questioning about what something is. It is too vague, lacking any organization. There is no dialogue or use of good vocabulary. This paper could have been assured of a **1** if the author had just once mentioned the locked door.

Narrative — Example #11

This example is a well-written narrative. I would score this a **high**. The author develops the beginning, fills the middle with description and detail about the contents of the rooms, and wraps it all up nicely at the end. Although there is no dialogue, the chronological order is clear, the vocabulary is good ("modernized," stunned") and even spelled correctly in most cases. The writer even uses strong verbs ("Paintings appeared on the walls."). What keeps this example from earning the highest score is the use of only simple sentences, the lack of dialogue, and a lack of "pizzazz." It is a perfect example of a **5** paper on a scale of 1-6, well-written but not outstanding.

Narrative — Example #12

While this writer cannot spell very well, all of his/her words are decipherable ("dargon"). Chronologically, the story flows well from entry into the room to meeting the trees and the ghost and finally returning home. The writer even wraps it up wondering if his/her mother knew about dragons. There is dialogue, and sentence structure varies despite the lack of commas. Strong verbs abound ("Shiver ran," "bird flew," "door slammed"). The vocabulary is excellent ("lumbered"). Since mechanics are the least important part of a score, and the story is well written, this would score a **high**, probably even the highest possible score due to its content, originality, clear organization, details, and focus on the topic at hand.

Narrative — Example #13

This is a basic medium paper. It has a beginning, a middle with some detail, and a definite ending. It has some attempts at good vocabulary ("extarodnary," "fantastick") and paragraphing. The writer clearly follows a chronological order, going into the door, going down the tunnel, finding the park, trying the rides, and finally trying the video games. The run-on sentences, however, interfere with the understanding of the paper, and that keeps it from receiving a higher score.

Narrative — Example #14

This student tried to write an expository essay, complete with transitions in the middle paragraphs, out of a narrative topic. While it has a definite beginning, middle, and end, and it does try to tell a story, the end is unclear. The author uses conversation (the phone calls) but parts are unexplained. (Who is Mrs. Stallbom, for example?) This paper would receive a **low** to **medium** score, due to the lack of clarity and the obvious essay format in a narrative paper.

5. Persuasive/Point of View Examples

TOPIC: "Should Community Service be a requirement for high school graduation?"

NOTE: Because scoring differs from state to state, these samples are scored **HIGH**, **MEDIUM**, **LOW**, or **ZERO** for ease of translation.

Sample Set #5
Persuasive/Point of View — "Community Service"

Example #1

For many years it has been proposed that high school students be forced to do community service in order to graduate. This is outrageous! Why put kids in situations like that. It's forced labor. "Well, kids always are asking to be treated like adults," you might tell us, but let me tell you, the only adults who are forced into working without pay are convicts! Teens need time, time for things like homework, or activities to unwind after a hard day at school, plus it's just dumb for us to do what is essentially forced labor (no pay). Besides, what would happen if we got hurt on the job? I really doubt we would be compensated.

First of all, students like me have absolutely no time during the week or on the weekend for community service. Last year, I was in band which met every day after school untill November. Then, the day before band got out, I had soccer tryouts. I got on the team and practiced every day after school for the soccer season. Then, a week before soccer was done, I began basketball. In all, I only came home right after school about a total of three weeks (21 days)! When I wasn't at school, I was either studying or sleeping. I know for a fact that this is how some kids live their lives (yes, there are others besides me), and believe me, there is no time for community service in our busy schedules.

Second of all, its just stupid for us to be forced into doing something and not get a reward. To me it seems like we would be on the same level as a convict, only without the bright orange clothes! We would be working with no pay to get out of this hell hole, only to go to another one for even less of a reward (not even any learning).

Last of all, what would happen if we were to get hurt and couldn't go to school for a few weeks? Would we be compensated? I really don't think we would. How would we make up the school work AND the community service we missed? Could we? It would be physically impossible to do so.

In conclusion, its clear that we would have no time, no pay, and could really, if injured, lose out on a lot. I think community service is a dumb requirement for all these reasons (and many more as well), and should not be required for high school graduation.

Sample Set #5
Persuasive/Point of View — "Community Service"

Example #2

Should be Requirement

Community Service is a great requirement because you learn a lot of respect and responsability for your actions. Community Service makes you open your eyes to real life.

Requirement of community service I say "yes why not." Community service for a punichment is a great idea. It gives something that who or what did the crime a dose of reality of life. It also gives what they take or breake back by the time they finish.

Jobs. Jobs. Jobs. Community service is a job, not a paying job, but a job. You get experiens in what ever you are doing or selling for that matter you also get experiens in.

What ever you are doing or selling for that matter you also get perseverence is a big part in having a job or geting the job.

Community service is March of Dimes help make healther babys. With March of dimes you get payed not with money or prizes but you get payed by knowing you saved a life.

The Salvashon Army is another exampel of community service.

So in my conclushon I say "yes" to community services not for the fact that it is a good punichment or good job experiens or to have good refrens but for the fact of knowing that a life was saved or some one is not alone or even frezing. So yes community service should be a requirement so you get a dose of realyty of life.

Sample Set #5
Persuasive/Point of View — "Community Service"

Example #3

Community Service Essay

Now, first off, don't get me wrong. I'm not saying I hate community service completly. But, I think that doing it under different circumstances would be better for many a people if they weren't told "There it is. Go do it!"

Alright, we have schools saying that you won't be allowed to graduate unless you have so and so amount of hours of community service, but for some people that's really hard because they might already have a job that <u>pays</u> and you'll have to cut your hours down (a lot!). Then where is the money going to come from? Also, what if they tell you a certin day for community service but your already working and you miss work, gee! You can be fired!

Another reason would be that, what about all the jobless people who could use more work? Just out of curiosity!

I guess, some other reasons (got to think or Mr. Owens will say I can't correctly elaborate!) would be that, if you get injured you won't be insured by a business, can't get worker's comp. (If it's an expensive doctor's bill).

There's lots of things like this that would make people (and should) skeptical! (Just because you got to think with caution.) Like I said before though. I'm not saying it's a bad thing, but every option should be explored!

Sample Set #5
Persuasive/Point of View — "Community Service"

Example #4

Community Service

I think that if your doing community hours you should get paid because you'll probably be out there from sun till it's dawn and that's really some long hours without getting paid for it and that's hard work all the day long with no money. I don't think most people will fall for it because as you see there's no pay what so ever and that is probably about the thing and probably to lazy to work.

I think the judges probably be letting people off a little easy because instead of going to jail over little of nothing, but it probably need to be issued for students to graduate but like I said some people won't do it without pay and don't get me wrong some will do it to get there diploma, but I think if they give an order most of the students probably would do it if it is consider for graduation.

Sample Set #5
Persuasive/Point of View — "Community Service"

Example #5

Community Service

Should community service be required to graduate from high school? Community service is a good thing for those of us that can afford to do it, but many of us can't and it would only make graduating a harder task, as if it's not hard already.

First of all, many students don't have the time to volunteer their time. Going to school five days a week gives you a lot of homework and can drain you of your energy. With the free time I do have I'm either studying or trying to catch up on some of my sleep. I beleive if I lost the little free time I do have I would fall behind in school.

Second of all, many can't afford to work for free. Not everyone's parents can afford to send their child to college or buy them a car. Many high school students hold a job so they can have a car or save for college. Community service would take away from your job, which would take away money, which would not allow you to have the things or the savings you want.

Thirdly, many students have a hard time graduating as it is. By having to have so many hours of community service it would make graduating harder and the whole process longer. Many student's can just <u>not</u> do it. Not because they don't want to, but because they really can't.

In conclusion, I think it just would not be a good idea. Let people choose to do community service. More people would be willing to do good at what ever it was they were doing if they were able to choose. If you force someone to do something they are just going to push away and not do their best. Community service. I beleive it should be someone's choice.

Sample Set #5
Persuasive/Point of View — "Community Service"

Example #6

Community Service

I think that community service is great, but I don't think it should be a requirement to graduate from high school. I don't know about everybody else, but I don't have enough time as it is, much less having enough to perform community service. It also seems like a punishment. And, I think that we should be encouraged to do community service, but not forced.

To start of with, I don't have enough time now to get everything and do everything I need to. When I get home the first thing I do is get ready to go to work. And then when I get home around six o'clock, I do my homework. Then if I have time, I like to lift weights. And, that's not all the time-management problems! What about sports? I have a real hard time getting off work for important sports events much less community service. If I was forced to do community service, there is no way I'd have enough time to get everything done.

Secondly, whenever I think of community service it always reminds me of when my sister got three speeding tickets, and as a punishment they gave her community service. It's almost as if we are being treated like criminals. Why should the school board require of upstanding high school students what the penal system requires of those who break the law. What message is that giving us? Community service is great for volunteers and criminals who need to pay back society, but it should not be a requirement to graduate from high school.

Last of all, I think that to force a high school student who is struggling to maintain good grades to do anything non-educational is wrong. If I did have time, I would be more than glad to help the community in some way, but right now I have to concentrate on my future, and most importantly on my education. And, I don't see that doing community service would help me in any way at this point in my life. Now this may sound selfish, but when I'm done with college and have a good, steady job, then I'll do a lot if community service. I believe in giving to those who are less fortunate than I am.

In conclusion, I would like to restate something I said earlier in this paper. "Community service is a great thing, but it should be encouraged not forced or required." I say this because we students have a lack of time, look on forced work as punishment, and need to concentrate on our future. Community service? Not now, thanks.

Sample Set #5
Persuasive/Point of View — "Community Service"

Example #7

Sure, No Problem

Community service to me is a very good thing to me. This kind of work is the best kind, because 9 times out of 10 your doing it from the heart. Community service should not be something demanding or stressful, but something you realy care about.

First, it makes better people. An example of a person becoming better with themselfs. Say that a person has to team up with somebody different from his race, for community service, and as time goes on they become good friends.

Second, community service comes from the heart and is a good thing because of that. For example I like to work with little kids and it comes from my heart and I feel good about myself.

In conclushun, community service to me is a good thing to me.   I like it. You will to.

Sample Set #5
Persuasive/Point of View — "Community Service"

Example #8

No Community Service

I think needing community service to graduat is quite wrong. What dose it show you did your parents haft to do it to graduat. Hear are my reasons I think us students shoud not haft to do it.

Time, why shoud we waste are time to do community service to graduat. My last year in high school I don't want to do community service, I whant to have fun. Students need to study, and be able to do there homework or project. Some students have job's and where can they find the time to fit this in to there schedel. Now this leads up to my next example.

Grads. All students that whant to go to college, haft to make the best grads they can, and shoud not haft to do the service to gratuat. You haft to do homework to pass any class, and doing this service takes time away from doing your homework.

But hear is the mane question in my mind, Why! Why shoud we haft to do this, you know your parents did not haft to do this, so why shoud we haft to do it to graduat. What do us students get out of it, so the city dose not haft to pay a person to do it, so a bissnes owner dose not haft to pay another persen to do work when you can get it for free.

Sample Set #5
Persuasive/Point of View — "Community Service"

Example #9

Down with Community Service

In my opinion requiring community service for graduation would just end up being a waste of time for everyone. For the students it would be a waste because they have busy schedules to complete that include work as well as school work. And for the manager it would be a waste because they'll have to take time out helping and showing students how things work. They'll waste even more time yelling at them to stay on task and do their job right. (You know teenagers. We need to be nagged or we get lazy!)

I personally think students have enough to worry about without community service. We need to keep our grades up. Senior years are usually pretty hectic with trying to find a good college to accept you and getting the grades to meet the requirements of the college. I know last year (9th grade) I started working towards a volleyball scholarship, but I could hardly stay on the team with a 1.9 grade point average. To get into most colleges you need at least a 3.0, so studying should be a top priority, and community service would definitely cut in on studying time.

A second reason community service should be forgotten about is the quality of work. If some is not going to get paid for their job, they're not going to work as hard, no matter what job it is. And if someone gets stuck doing something they really hate, they'll hardly put any effort into it. (If they're lucky, a friend will be there and they can both get screamed at together.) One of my friend's mom hates her job so much she sits at work thinking of ways to get fired. This doesn't help anyone much.

Working for free would not only waste the students time, but whoever they're working for as well. Someone's going to have to show the "fresh fish" how things work around there, and someone's going to have to help them when they screw up.

Transportation is another problem that could occur, and one day your worker just might not show up which would put you on the spot and possible waste more of your time looking for a replacement. If a student has another job already, working times may collide, and that's going to waste a lot of someone's time working that mess out (plus it might cause the student to get fired from their paying job.)

In conclusion I feel the community service requirement to graduate is selfishly organized and inappropriate. Students have too much other stuff to worry about like how to pay off their car. They need to concentrate on grades. And, the bosses will lose time as well. A community service requirement for graduation is a lose—lose proposition.

Sample Set #5
Persuasive/Point of View — "Community Service"

Example #10

Community Service Should be a Part of Graduation Requirement

I think Community Service should be a Graduation Requirement. It it was you would still be learning, but you would only be on the outside of the school. Thats were most students wish they was anyway.

The first reason would be to learn not to throw paper on the ground. If you or anyone else throw paper on the ground you don't want to pick it up. Do you think someone else wants to clean up behind you. You're not just doing something for yourself but for your community. You would also be proud that you made the community look better.

The second reason is you may found some interesting things. You may find a comic book that's worth some money. Someone might find a purse that needs returning to the owner. You may even find some money.

Last, but not lease. You may learn how to keep your home clean. Like if you was looking for a paper on your desk but you can't find it because your desk was to funky. One morning you was late for work and you was looking for something to wear so you put on the first suit you see but didn't know it wasn't clean. Then all day long you smelled like roadkill that's been dead for months. You could have visitors but you wont let them in because you haven't seen what your floor look like in 4 or 5 months. All of these things wouldn't have happened if you wouldn't have taken just one more class for graduation.

So see if you take this class it wouldn't hurt. You would learn things and keep your house up better. So say no to P.I.S. and yes to C.S.C.

Sample Set #5
Persuasive/Point of View — "Community Service"

Example #11

Essay

When I first thought about it. I said that there shouldn't have to have community service for graduation. Then I thought about it again. Then I said yes we should have it because we need to learn how to work. And start helping older people and sick people out. More then that will learn the value of money. And will also learn many trades. I will be more focus and responsabile toward life. Thats my argument.

Sample Set #5
Persuasive/Point of View — "Community Service"

Example #12

Community service should not be a requirement to graduate. People work to get enough credits to graduate and keep up their grades and they don't need to have another thing that they have to do. It is something that kids should want to do, not have to do. It is also criminal-like treatment and time consuming.

First of all, it is not going to help the community any if they are forcing people who don't want to help to help. There are plenty of people who love to volunteer and they should be the one's doing it. If you are forced to do anything, you are not going to want to do it. Kids who are pushed into it unwillingly are never going to be helping again because of the bad experience. Some people may like helping after having to, but they could have found that out willingly.

Secondly, isn't community service a punishemnt to criminals? We should be rewarded for going to school, not be forced to do something convicts do. You might have well have stole something and been sentenced to 20 hours of community service if it was required. The only thing missing is some jail time.

Finally it would take up a lot of time. It may sound selfish, but a lot of kids are balancing a hard schedule and it may be hard to fit that in. They could be making money to support themselves with that time. Kids nowadays have a lot of responsibilities, and it would be hard to do that.

In conclusion, it is always good to help out your community and it should be voluntary and not like it was a punishment. It should be something good and you wouldn't want people with bad attitudes doing it.

Sample Set #5
Persuasive/Point of View — "Community Service"

Example #13

Essay

I think community service shouldn't be a graduation requiremnt to get out of high school.

The first reason I don't think it shouldn't be one is because you are going to help the city out and the city doesn't try to help you out with nothing but try to give the people in the city hard time. Then they ask them to do something for the city. But most of the time when the people of city go down town to city hall they try to be nasty to the people and give them a hard time.

For another reason I think it shouldn't be a requirement is because when you do it you don't get a grade for it or you don't get a credit for it and it doesn't teach nothing that is going to help you down the road of life.

For the last final reason I think it shouldn't be a requirement is because you are working without pay. That is not fair because the people that you are working or watching over you when you are working are getting paid but you are not that is not fair. You are doing it for free but if you call the city to do something they would like you to work for free.

Those are the reasons I think it shouldn't be a requirement for graduation.

Sample Set #5
Persuasive/Point of View — "Community Service"

Example #14

Community service should not be a graduation requirement. Students barely have enough time for homework now, let alone if we needed to go volunteer somethere. Weekends should be reserved for fun or relaxation or catch up from the five day week, and time spent on sports and after school jobs make community service impossible to serve. Please, we high school students don't need another requirement for graduation. Enough!

When we get home from school, a majority of the students have at least two hours of homework to complete, sometimes more. After that, who would feel like doing community service? Besides that, our parents are usually working and unless you're within walking distance to somewhere to volunteer, you don't have any transportation. Also students need to study (above and beyond the homework) for upcoming tests and quizzes. Time, like a diamond, is precious.

The second reason we shouldn't have community service for a graduation requirement is because we would need to do it on the weekends as well as during the school week. Weekends, apart from catching up on any homework or studying for upcoming tests, are made for fun and relaxation from the rigors of the school week. This does not mean just hanging out with your friends (like most adults think), but also to catch up on sleep (definitely lacking during the school week) and to relax from the pressures of school. It is a catch up time for our bodies and our minds, not to mention for any homework hanging over our heads.

Thirdly, a lot of students have after school sports, which would leave no or little time for community service. Plus after you're done with your sports, you're too tired to go volunteer. And, even if you dragged yourself to volunteer after playing sports for two hours, then you would have no energy left to do your homework. You would just want to go home and sleep. Sports aren't the only problem with after school community service. Some students who, because their parents are not rich, have to work after school would never find the time to volunteer. It's not fair to penalize those students and keep them from graduating. Most students who work do so because they have to, not because they want to. They now don't have enough time for their paying jobs, let alone volunteer work. There just aren't enough hours in the day for high school students to fit in community service.

In conclusion, community service shouldn't be a graduation requirement. We have too much going on to worry about volunteering. We wouldn't have enough time to devote to homework, our weekends would be all work and no play, and after school sports or work may have to be cancelled totally to make the time to complete the community service requirement for graduation. I say, "No" to community service. Enough is enough!

Scores and Analyses for Sample Set #5

Persuasive/Point of View — "Community Service"

Persuasive/Point of View — Example #1

I score this paper a **high**. It is fairly well written, stays on the topic, gives examples (the writer's hectic life in soccer and basketball), uses good vocabulary ("compensated," "proposed"). While there are no similes, sentence structure is varied. There is even a quote at the beginning. Mechanics and usage errors do not abound. On the writing assessment, this paper probably would not receive the top score. It could not earn a higher score. It is a really good paper, but it is not outstanding.

Persuasive/Point of View — Example #2

The problem with this example is that it is more expository than persuasive. The writer explains what community service is ("Community service is March of Dimes") instead of arguing for or against requiring community service for graduation. The writer goes on in this vein for four paragraphs. Mechanics, usage, and spelling errors sometimes interfere with the meaning of the paper (look at paragraphs #2 and #3). The writer gives one attempt at using good vocabulary ("perseverence"). Organization is haphazard, however. Because the writer does mention the topic in the first and last paragraphs and lists one or two arguments (with little support), the paper would score at least a **1** on the writing assessment.

Persuasive/Point of View — Example #3

This paper does stay on the topic in all but the one place he/she addresses her teacher, but support is poor. The conclusion is vague and doesn't really make sense in the context of the prompt ("every option should be explored"). The writer uses a few good vocabulary words ("elaborate," "skeptical") albeit incorrectly spelled. This is a good **low medium** essay because of its lack of support and more than average number of errors ("your" instead of "you're" and the lack of commas, for example).

Persuasive/Point of View — Example #4

This paper is expository not persuasive. The student does not address the topic and instead talks about how important it is to get paid for community service. I don't quite understand the part about the judges. There is no apparent organization at all. The writer jumps from one topic to another. The only sentence that mentions communitity service as a requirement for graduation is the last one, and it does not make much sense. This paper is also replete with mechanical and spelling errors, but the lack of focus is what makes it **unscorable** or a bare-minimum score.

Persuasive/Point of View — Example #5

This is a perfect **medium** paper. The student stays on the topic, gives three arguments, has an adequate introduction and conclusion, uses adequate vocabulary, includes adequate support (although the argument in paragraph #4 falls apart), and writes fairly well. Spelling errors ("beleive") never get in the way of comprehension. Transitions begin each middle paragraph. All the elements are there, but it is in no way outstanding enough or well-enough written to earn a higher score.

Persuasive/Point of View — Example #6

This well-written paper deserves a **high** score. On the actual test, it probably would receive the highest or next-to-highest score, depending on the judges. The paper never strays from the topic. Its organization is clear. The arguments are well-thought out. Transitions begin the middle paragraphs. Vocabulary is excellent ("penal," "upstanding"), and mechanical errors are few. The support is specific and thorough as when the author talks in paragraph #2 about his evening (homework, lifting weights). It is, on the whole, an excellent essay, written with flair and conviction.

Persuasive/Point of View — Example #7

This essay is **unscorable**. It is not a persuasive essay trying to give arguments as to why community service should or should not be a requirement for graduation. In fact, it never mentions graduation at all. This expository essay is an explanation of why community service "to me is a very good thing to me." Organization is also muddled although there is an introduction and conclusion of sorts. There are numerous mechanical and spelling errors but, as in Example #4, the bottom line is staying on the topic. This essay does not. Some judges might give this paper a **1** because it does mention community service.

Persuasive/Point of View — Example #8

Apart from the egregious and numerous spelling errors in every line (this student may be dislexic in spelling) and numerous mechanical errors, this writer does, except in the last paragraph, stay on the topic. There is an introduction and conclusion, though only one transition is used, and there are two paragraphs with arguments against community service. There is very little development of the arguments, however, and there is no elaboration, just a list ("I whant to have fun. Students need to study , and be able to do there homework or project. Some students have job's and where can they find the time"). For all these reasons, this essay would score a **low** on the writing assessment.

Persuasive/Point of View — Example #9

This essay, obviously, deserves a **high** score, but not the highest. Except for the end of the third paragraph, the writer stays on the topic. The paper has humor ("You know teenagers...."), good vocabulary ("inappropriate," "proposition"), good support in the middle paragraphs, and, clever use of transitions. It is clearly well organized and contains only a few errors. It would not receive the highest score because, while it is a very good paper, it is not outstanding, and support flags a little in paragraph three.

Persuasive/Point of View — Example #10

The point of this essay is unclear. Is the student talking about keeping your community and house clean or about requiring community service for graduation? And the end, what do "P.I.S." and "C.S.C." mean? The student talks about reasons ("The first reason") but then strays from the topic by going off on a tangent ("Do you think someone else wants to clean up behind you."). Spelling errors don't get in the way of comprehension, but sometimes punctuation errors do. While this is organized in the main topics, the sub topics wander off. Because of all these problems, this paper would score **low**. It probably would not earn the lowest score on the actual test because of the organization and focus.

Persuasive/Point of View — Example #11

This paper is clearly a **low**. It could not earn higher than a **1** on the actual test because of the lack of development. It does stay on the topic, but it is simply a list of reasons why community service should be required for graduation. There is no support at all, no introduction, no varied sentence structure, no good vocabulary usage, and only a one sentence conclusion.

Persuasive/Point of View — Example #12

This is a perfect **medium** paper. It is a good paper that stays the topic, has an obvious organization with transitions, provides support for the three arguments, and does not have an excessive number of errors. All in all, it is a average paper. The support in the first paragraph is good, but the other two are a bit weaker. The conclusion is skimpy. Vocabulary is adequate. It is, in short, an O.K. but in no way outstanding essay.

Persuasive/Point of View — Example #13

This paper mentions the word "community service" in the first and last paragraphs and uses "it" everywhere else so meaning is sometimes confused. The writer gets off the topic a few times, talking about the "nasty" people at city hall. The end of the fourth paragraph doesn't make sense, and all of the support for the arguments falls apart. There is only a one sentence introduction and conclusion. Vocabulary is adequate. This is a **low medium** essay because of the confusing sentences and lack of support.

Persuasive/Point of View — Example #14

This essay is really good. It is clearly a **high** paper and probably would earn the top score on the actual test. It never strays from the topic. Organization is clear. Three arguments are well developed with lots of details and specific support. The writer even includes humor in the asides in the third paragraph. Vocabulary is excellent ("upcoming," "devote," "lacking"), and sentence structure is varied. There is a minimum of errors. There is even a simile (albeit a trite one). This is a good example of an outstanding persuasive essay.

Bibliography

References

Caplan, Rebakah, and Deech, Catherine. *Showing Writing - Training Program to Help Students Be Specific*. Berkeley: University of California Press, 1980.

Florida Writes! Report on the 1992 Eighth Grade Field Test. Tallahassee: Department of Education, 1992.

Florida Writes! Report on the 1993 Assessment. Tallahassee: Department of Education, 1993, grades 4, 8.

Florida Writes! Report on the 1994 Assessment. Tallahassee: Department of Education, 1994, grades 4, 8, 10.

Florida Writes! Report on the 1995 Assessment. Tallahassee: Department of Education, 1995, grades 4, 8, 10.

Florida Writes! Report on the 1996 Assessment. Tallahassee: Department of Education, 1996, grades 4, 8, 10.

Florida Writes! Report on the 1997 Assessment. Tallahassee: Department of Education, 1997, grades 4, 8, 10.

Florida Writes! Report on the 1998 Assessment. Tallahassee: Department of Education, 1998, grades 4, 8, 10.

Florida Writes! Report on the 1999 Assessment. Tallahassee: Department of Education, 1999, grades 4, 8, 10.

Forney, Melissa. *The Writing Menu*. Gainesville: Maupin House, 1999.

Freeman, Marcy. *Listen to This*. Gainesville: Maupin House Publishing, 1996.

Kiester, Jane. *Caught'ya! Grammar with a Giggle*. Gainesville: Maupin House Publishing, 1990.

Kiester, Jane. *Caught'ya Again! More Grammar with a Giggle*. Gainesville: Maupin House Publishing, 1993.

Kiester, Jane. *The Chortling Bard! Grammar with a Giggle for High Schools*. Gainesville: Maupin House Publishing, 1997.

Kiester, Jane. *Elementary, My Dear! Part I — Grammar with a Giggle for Grades One, Two, and Three*. Gainesville: Maupin House Publishing, 2000.

Sparks, J. E. *Write for Power*, Manhattan Beach, CA: Communication Associates, 1995.

Books Used for Examples for Practice of Types of Writing

Angelou, Maya. *I Know Why the Caged Bird Sings*. New York: Bantam Books, 1971.

Milne, A. A. *Winnie the Pooh*. New York: American Book-Stratford Press, Inc., 1954.

Rowlings, J. K. *Harry Potter and the Sorcerer's Stone*. New York: Scholastic, Inc., 1998.

White, E. B. *Charlotte's Web*. New York: Harper Brothers, 1952.

If you enjoyed
Blowing Away the State Writing Assessment Test by Jane Bell Kiester, try these, too.

Caught'ya! Grammar with a Giggle
Jane Bell Kiester

Teach grammar, usage, mechanics, and vocabulary in context with this classic sentence-a-day book of age-appropriate, humorous soap operas. One story each for elementary, middle, and high school, each of which can be easily adapted to fit your classroom's specific needs. Each story has enough sentences for a whole school year. Includes machine-readable tests, plot outlines, and spin-off activities. A great resource for building basic skills and raising writing scores. Tens of thousands of public, private, and home-school teachers agree that this technique works. 227 pp. 0-929895-04-5. #MH07. **$17.95.**

Caught'ya Again! More Grammar with a Giggle
Jane Bell Kiester

Holy Moldy Bread contest! Kiester strikes again, this time with four more stories plus mini-lessons, writing workshops, and a complete grammar primer. These zany, creative stories teach solid skills that will transform your students into better writers. One easily adapted story each for elementary, middle, and high school. Teacher keys, tests, and special notes for home-school teachers are included. A great time-saver that works! 314 pp. 0-929895-09-6. #MH06. **$17.95.**

The Chortling Bard: Caught'ya! Grammar with a Giggle for High School
Jane Bell Kiester

Do your high schoolers become a pack of **mammering joltheads** when you try to teach them grammar and mechanics? Do they get all **onion-eyed** when you tell them to pull out their handbooks and primers? **Bestill** their **beslubbering mewls** — the popular Caught'ya! technique for teaching grammar and mechanics has taken a Shakespearean twist especially for high school! Kiester transforms three of the Bard's plays into adaptable Caught'ya! sentences for high school students at any level. Includes a mix and match menu of Elizabethan swear words, enough Caught'ya! sentences for **three** school years, a straight-spoken grammar handbook, and exams (with keys) for midterms and the end of the year. 240 pp. 0-929895-25-8. #MH41. **$19.95.**

Elementary My Dear! Caught'ya! Grammar with a Giggle for Grades 1, 2, and 3
Jane Bell Kiester

Build basic skills in context and you'll enhance early success in language arts. These one-sentence-a-day soap-opera stories teach grade-appropriate grammar, mechanics, usage, and vocabulary with humor and fun. One story each for Grades 1, 2, and 3. Includes a single-classroom-use CD with the complete text of each story, ready to be copied to overheads or for handouts. 288 pp. 0-929895-30-4. #MH56. **$23.95.**

(Over, Please)

Listen to This: Developing an Ear for the Expository
Marcia S. Freeman

Model one of the 18 short, well written expository pieces to your class, then discuss the elements of writing craft with the help of the model, teaching notes, and an expository primer. Samples include newspaper and magazine articles, letters to the editor, poems, essays, and process descriptions. 132 pp. 0-929895-19-3. #MH30. **$17.95.**

Listen to This plus Overhead Transparency Masters
Eighteen ready-to-copy overhead transparency masters (formatted in large print, one sample to a page, and hole-punched for easy storage). A great way to display the Read-Aloud Samples to your students. For single classroom use. Includes one copy of *Listen to This*. #MH50. **$23.95.**

Dynamite Writing Ideas: Empowering Students to Become Authors
Melissa Forney

Dynamite Writing Ideas supports your writing program with ideas, strategies, and handy reproducibles that save you time — from August setup through end-of-the-year publishing. Perfect for teachers who have always wanted to integrate writing workshops into their classrooms, but didn't know where to begin. 124 pp. 0-929895-18-5. #MH29. **$17.95.**

The Writing Menu: Ensuring Success for Every Student
Melissa Forney

Tired of grading stacks of essays that were all written in response to the same prompt? *The Writing Menu* shows you a better way! Learn how to present customizable assignments to your K-6 students so they can write to their own cultural backgrounds, learning styles, and personal interests. Includes grade-appropriate Target Skills, composing techniques, and assignment ideas. Emphasizes expository and narrative genres. 132 pp. 0-929895-33-9. #MH49. **$14.95.**

Building a Writing Community: A Practical Guide
Marcia S. Freeman

If you want to create a community of writers who love to write and speak the language of writers, you'll love this book. The classroom-tested techniques satisfy young writers' need for structure and content while offering them freedom to develop their style, repertoire and voice. More than 350 models, lessons, procedures, and activities help schools and districts teach writing effectively. Includes 37 reproducibles. 242 pp. 0-929895-13-4. #MH24. **$23.95.**

Voice Lessons: Classroom Activities to Teach Diction, Detail, Imagery, Syntax, and Tone
Nancy Dean

Prepare your high school students for AP, IB, and other standardized tests that demand an understanding of the subtle elements that comprise an author's unique voice. Each of the 100 sharply focused, historically and culturally diverse passages from world literature targets a specific component of voice, presenting the elements in short, manageable exercises that function well as class openers. Includes teacher notes and discussion suggestions. 160 pp. 0-929895-35-5. #MH62. **$19.95.**

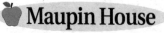 **Maupin House**

Contact Maupin House for quality on-site professional training. Free catalog. Phone: 1-800-524-0634 or 352-373-5588
E-mail: info@maupinhouse.com or visit www.maupinhouse.com. Checks, VISA/MC, or purchase orders accepted.

About the Author

Jane Kiester is the author of the popular *Caught'ya!* books: *Caught'ya! Grammar with a Giggle*; *Caught'ya Again! More Grammar with a Giggle*; *The Chortling Bard! Grammar with a Giggle for High School*; and *Elementary, My Dear! Grammar with a Giggle for Grades 1, 2, and 3*, all published by Maupin House. Teachers all over the country also use her third book, *Blowing Away the State Writing Assessment Test*, to help improve their students' scores on state writing assessment tests. Jane currently is writing three new books.

In addition to writing books, Jane has given hundreds of workshops to fellow teachers around the country for the past ten years. Her subject? The same as in her classroom where she happily has taught elementary and middle school for over 30 years — teaching students to write well.

During her many years as a classroom teacher, Jane has served as Grade-level Chairperson and as the chairperson of various departments. She is also a past President of the Alachua County Teachers of English. Jane has been recognized four times by *Who's Who Among America's Teachers*. In 2002 she won Teacher of the Year for her school and Middle School Teacher of the Year for her county.